HOW TO
ENGLISH

EVERYTHING YOU NEED TO MASTER ENGLISH

HOW TO ENGLISH

31 DAYS TO BE AN INDEPENDENT LEARNER

Adam David Broughton

How To English

Copyright © 2019 by Adam David Broughton

All rights reserved.

Edited by Jennifer Renart

Cover and book design by Vincent Vi

No part of this book may be reproduced in any form or by any electronic or mechanical means, including information storage and retrieval systems, without permission in writing from the author, except by a reviewer who may quote brief passages in a review.

www.how-to-english.com

A FREE WORKBOOK ACCOMPANIES THIS BOOK.

HOW TO ENGLISH
31 DAYS TO BE AN INDEPENDENT LEARNER
THE FREE WORKBOOK

The workbook contains additional activities for each of the practice exercises covered in this book.

Available for free at www.how-to-english.com/workbook

Get your copy today to get the most out of this book.

*For every student I have ever taught, without whom
this book would never have been written.
Together, you taught me more than I could ever teach you.*

CONTENTS

Preface 1

Introduction 5

PART I THE FUNDAMENTAL BASICS

Day 1	How to Find Time to Practise English	27
Day 2	How to Take Control of Your English Learning	35
Day 3	How to Organise What You Learn	43
Day 4	How to Improve Fluency	49
Day 5	How to Master Fluency	57
Day 6	How to Master Listening for Specific Information – The Absolute Best Listening Exercise You Can Do	67
Day 7	How to Learn by Listening – It All Starts With Listening	75
Day 8	Motivation, Self-Discipline and Habits (Part 1) – How to Think in The Long Term	85

PART II HOW TO MAKE EVERYTHING YOU LEARN RELEVANT

Day 9	How to Practise Properly	99
Day 10	How to Make Everything You Learn 100% Relevant to YOU	107
Day 11	How to Find Questions and Doubts	117
Day 12	How to Stop Making Mistakes – Good Mistakes and Bad Mistakes	127
Day 13	How to Know If You Are Making a Mistake	137
Day 14	How to Learn From Every Text You Read and Everything You Listen to	145
Day 15	How to Identify Your Weakness – What's Your Biggest Weakness?	155
Day 16	Motivation, Self-Discipline and Habits (Part 2) – How to Always Be Motivated	163

PART III HOW TO MASTER VOCABULARY, GRAMMAR AND PRONUNCIATION

Day 17	How to Read Books in English	175
Day 18	How to Increase Your Working Vocabulary	185
Day 19	How to Understand and Use Grammar Correctly	195
Day 20	How to Have Perfect Grammar	207
Day 21	How to Improve Your Pronunciation in English	217
Day 22	How to Never Be Misunderstood When Speaking in English	229
Day 23	How to Improve Your Memory – Remember Everything You Learn in English	239
Day 24	Motivation, Self-Discipline and Habits (Part 3) – How to Improve Your Self-Discipline	251

PART IV PLANNING FOR THE FUTURE: HOW TO BECOME AN INDEPENDENT ENGLISH LEARNER

Day 25	How to Improve Your Weakness – The One Thing That English Learners Rarely Do	265
Day 26	How to Plan And Reach Your Goals	277
Day 27	How to Create and Complete Your Own Intensive Course	285
Day 28	How to Make Short-Term, Mid-Term and Long-Term Goals	295
Day 29	How to Control What You Learn And How You Learn	305
Day 30	Motivation, Self-Discipline and Habits (Part 4) – How to Create a Habit	317
Day 31	How to Put It All Together	327

PREFACE

Well done for buying this book.

You've just walked half the journey. When you finally decide that now is the time to make progress and now is the time to take control of your learning, you instantly get past the most difficult part of learning.

What is this book about?

To answer that question, I first need to tell you why I wrote this book.

I wrote this book as a solution to the biggest and most common problem that every English learner faces at some point. That problem is frustration.

It starts when they stop making progress in English. It gets worse when their level starts to go down. Then they get desperate when nothing they do helps them improve.

Then they lose hope.

The fire in their belly disappears, they stop feeling motivated, and they think that someone else will help them improve. What they don't know is that nobody is coming to help them.

In order to make progress, you need that fire in your belly. That fire is the feeling that you have control over your own destiny. We humans are most motivated when we feel that our actions contribute to our own success. We are least motivated when we feel that we have no control over our own success; the feeling that someone else is deciding our destiny for us, and that there is nothing that we can do to help ourselves.

Let me tell you a story about taking control of your own destiny.

Many years ago during the second year of my teaching career, I had a class with two students that completely changed the way I teach.

These two students were Anton and Mohammed; one from Russia, the other from Yemen. Two absolute beginners.

It was winter in Brighton, England, which was not a very busy time of the year in the international English school I was teaching in. Anton and Mohammed were the only students in my A0 class.

The first class was how to greet people and introduce yourself, the alphabet and numbers. Progress was slow.

They had a lot in common. They were both the same age, both their families worked in the oil industry, and they were both learning English to be able to get a job in the industry.

After the first week, Anton started to attend fewer and fewer classes. He told me that he had joined the local golf club and was playing golf most days.

Mohammed attended class religiously. He was always on time, always did his homework and always made an effort.

As was expected, Mohammed finished the three-month course ready to start the next level, or even an A2 course if he pushed himself.

Anton ended the course with less than 50% attendance and never did his homework. When he did come to class, he asked me questions about grammar, vocabulary and expressions; things he had heard his new golf friends say.

He "finished the course" with a good B1+. He could have a conversation about any topic and had become a confident English speaker. From A0 to B1+.

In three months.

Let me tell you, three months in a country is not a long time. He used the time perfectly.

Mohammed was a great student and achieved what standard teaching practice told him he would achieve. Anton, however, took control of his own learning. He listened carefully to what native speakers said to him and what he read. He asked questions continuously about the language and filled his time with real-life practice.

The perfect recipe for learning a language.

That class taught me two very important lessons.

The first is that it's not what you do in English class that determines how much progress you make. It's what you do when you are *not* in class.

The second is that it isn't so important *what* you learn in English. What is more important is *how* you learn English. In other words, how you learn English is more important than what you learn in English.

I teach people *how to* learn English, not *what to* learn in English. I teach them how to take control of their English learning so that they can get the results they want.

I teach my students to be like Anton.

The good news is that making progress in English can be easy. The only problem is, you don't know *how to*.

And that is exactly what this book is about. I am going to teach you *how to* learn English. When you learn that, you find that you stop feeling frustrated with English and you start making more progress than ever.

When you learn *how to* learn, you never need to worry about *what* you learn.

It's time to stop feeling frustrated. It's time to take control of your English. It's time to start making the progress that you have always wanted.

I hope you enjoy reading this book as much as I did writing it, and I hope you enjoy the journey to English mastery.

INTRODUCTION

LEARNER FRUSTRATION

"Every human needs to be moving forward."

I love my job. I really do.

What's the best thing about my job?

The best thing about my job without any doubt is watching my students learn. When my students learn, I can see their faces respond to this new knowledge. When I teach my students something new or interesting, you can see little light bulbs lighting up in their heads. It's a great feeling and the reason I go back into the classroom every day.

But of course, every job has its pros and cons.

What's the worst thing about my job?

The worst thing about my job is what I call *learner frustration*. Unfortunately, it's something I see every day.

Learner frustration happens to every learner at some point, and it's not always a bad thing. Most of the time it can actually motivate you.

Here's an example.

I play the guitar. I've played the guitar since I was about fourteen or so. The learning process for the guitar has never been continuous progress. It's not linear. It's more like a set of stairs. Progress is flat and I don't improve, although I practise regularly. That makes me frustrated. Then suddenly, I move up a level. I jump up to the next step, and

I feel very motivated again. After a while, progress starts to go flat again. Then suddenly, I jump up another level. And the whole process repeats itself…

It's perfectly normal to feel frustrated sometimes. It's the normal learning process. It shows that you want to make progress, and it makes you work more and put more effort in so you can jump up a level again.

The problem is when you go a long time without making progress. This is when learner frustration can really start to have a negative impact on your learning.

In the example about me and the guitar, I experience learner frustration. However, it's not a big problem because it doesn't last very long. In fact, it can actually help me.

> **LEARNER FRUSTRATION STARTS TO BE VERY PROBLEMATIC WHEN IT LASTS FOR A LONG TIME.**

Imagine you have a headache. It feels bad, and you get frustrated and annoyed with the headache. But when the headache goes away, you feel great again and happy that you no longer have a headache.

Now imagine that headache doesn't go away. It becomes horrible and eventually, you start to think that it will never go away.

> **THEN YOU START TO LOSE HOPE.**

Maybe you even think that having a headache all the time is normal. The difference between an acute headache and a chronic headache can have drastic effects on your life.

And this is exactly what happens with chronic learner frustration.

Feeling frustrated at certain points in your learning journey is perfectly normal and can even help you feel motivated to improve.

Introduction

Feeling frustrated for a long period of time, just like a chronic headache, can completely change or even destroy your learning journey.

And the reason learners become frustrated in the first place is due to a lack of progress. Humans, in all situations, need to feel that they are making progress. Humans always need to be moving forward, moving towards something and making progress in that journey. If they feel they are not making progress, they become frustrated.

When you are frustrated for a long period of time, you start to lose hope.

And when there is no hope, those light bulbs in your head all turn off and it goes dark.

Many years ago I went to Thailand on holiday. One day, my friend and I went on an excursion to the jungle. I remember seeing a big elephant with a chain around its ankle. The chain was about 3 metres long and was attached to a small post that was stuck in the ground. The elephant was more than strong enough to pull the post out of the ground and go wherever it wanted to.

But it didn't.

It walked around the 3-metre radius that the length of the chain gave it.

I asked our guide why it didn't just pull the post out of the ground and walk away.

He explained, "It's the same post as when it was a baby. It will try to escape when it's small but it's not strong enough. After a while, it just accepts that it can't escape and stops trying."

The chain blocks the body when it's a baby, and blocks the mind when it's an adult.

Something very similar happens to frustrated English learners.

I see and speak to frustrated English learners every day. Each story is similar to all the others I have heard before. There is always a lack of progress. Frustrated learners have often lost hope. It's almost as if they are looking for a miracle. They are waiting for someone to help them make progress again.

But nobody is coming to help them.

It breaks my heart because I know that they are the only ones that can help them make progress again. They just don't know it.

I HAVE IDENTIFIED THREE TYPES OF LEARNER FRUSTRATION.

The first is when an English learner had a very good level in the past but, due to a lack of contact with the language, is slowly losing their level. I call this frustration *The Slow Death*.

I know, it doesn't sound nice!

The second is when an English learner achieved a good level by attending classes when they were younger. Now, they have a job, a family and other priorities. They only have two hours of classes per week that they attend at work. This learner frustration is called *Complete Stagnation*. This one is very common. The learner simply stays at the same level for years and years. This frustration is quite sad because the learner often accepts it. These learners are often what I call the *Perpetual Bs*, English learners that have a level B (intermediate) for years and years. They get trapped in that level and find it impossible to improve.

The third frustration is when an English learner goes on an intensive and their level improves. Then, when the course finishes, their level starts to go down again. After a year or so, they are back where they were before. But they have determination, so they go on another course. Their level improves again, but then the course finishes, and their level drops again. Every time they attend a course, their level improves. Every time they are not attending a course, their level goes down. Up and down, up and down. For obvious reasons, I call this frustration *The Rollercoaster*.

Each frustration has its own characteristics, but they all share one thing in common: a lack of progress. This lack of progress is what makes the learner frustrated. Remember, every human needs to be moving forward.

I see these frustrated learners everywhere and it's so sad.

It's sad because I know that their frustration is totally avoidable.

And that is why I decided to write this book.

I made it my mission to help frustrated English learners. The only thing I care about is that my English students improve their English.

Everything else is secondary.

All I want to do is help as many people as possible who are frustrated with their progress in English and feel that there is a better way of improving their level than the traditional route.

AND THERE IS A BETTER WAY.

Everything I do now as a teacher is to try to end learner frustration. I want to show English learners that there is no need for this frustration to exist. I want to show them that they have complete control over how much they learn, when they learn and what they learn.

Don't be like the elephant on a chain. Learn how to avoid frustration and you will be able to break the chain.

But first, we need to see where learner frustration comes from…

THE TWO BIG PROBLEMS WITH ENGLISH TEACHING

"You can go to a million English classes, but that doesn't mean you will improve your English."

There are two major problems with attending English classes to improve in English: *what* you learn and *how* you learn.

In this chapter, I'll explain the problem with *what* you learn.

Very often, a frustrated learner will complain about their lack of progress and say, "Adam, I've been having English classes for twenty years and I still have the same level!"

My reply is always the same: "You can go to a million English classes, but that doesn't mean you will improve."

The reason for this is that all learning comes from within.

Let me repeat that and write it in capitals because it's very important.

ALL LEARNING COMES FROM WITHIN.

The most common mistake about learning English is that we think learning comes from an external source: a teacher or a class.

100% OF ALL LEARNING HAPPENS IN YOUR OWN HEAD.

The teacher can show you something and the class can help, but it's only when something clicks in your own brain that you learn.

Nobody can *put* new information in your head.

All learning comes from within.

Let me explain.

Introduction

What does a teacher do?

"Erm...teach?"

Well done!

What does a teacher teach you?

"The teacher is the expert, so whatever they feel is necessary."

Here is the problem, "whatever they feel is necessary."

I've been teaching English learners from all over the world, at all levels, since 2005. I truly believe that if an English learner is starting from nothing, then absolutely, the best thing they can do to get a solid foundation is go to English classes.

In this case, "whatever the teacher feels is necessary" is totally relevant. Every good teacher knows exactly what an English learner needs when they start learning the language.

Having a solid foundation is essential.

LEARNING ENGLISH IS SIMILAR TO BUILDING A HOUSE.

Imagine you're going to build a house. Would you start building the house by laying the bricks directly onto the ground?

No, of course not. The house wouldn't stand for very long. All houses need strong foundations.

All English learners need a solid foundation. This foundation is the same for every English learner.

As teachers, we know what the basic needs are for ALL students, and will start by teaching them that.

However, once the foundations are done, what do you build onto it?

Each house is different; each learner is different. Each learner's needs start to diverge.

This is where the student should start to take control of their own learning. The problem is, because they've depended on a teacher for so long for their knowledge needs, they carry on as normal.

Likewise, the teacher is so used to their role that they continue to do the same thing they've always done, which is to be responsible for what the learner learns.

From B1 onwards, the learner and teacher should swap roles to maximise learning. The person that leads the class should not be the teacher, but the learner.

This does not happen in standard English teaching, though.

So the teacher continues doing what they've always done. However, as the learner progresses, the language that the teacher decides to teach starts to become less and less relevant.

This is because the teacher needs to teach to the masses, so the language they teach is aimed at the masses. That's why it's called "general English".

I think learners deserve more than "general".

Teaching general English at beginner levels is fine because everything you teach them will be relevant for all of them. The foundations of a language are the same for everybody.

As they progress, however, and each learner's individual needs start to differ, what the teacher teaches becomes less and less relevant for each individual student.

The learner then starts to make progress more slowly. Then progress starts to stagnate.

This is when the learner starts to feel frustrated and thinks, "I don't understand! I made so much progress when I started learning English, but the more I improve, the slower progress gets".

Introduction

Sound familiar?

The teacher can build a strong foundation for you and, to a certain extent, the walls of the house. Everything else, you, the learner, should decide on the finishing touches in the house.

After all, it's your house!

Do you want a carpet or tiled floor? Would you like curtains or blinds? What colour? Is a beautiful bathroom more important to you, or would you prefer a cosy living room? And so on, and so forth.

The list is almost endless because there are infinite ways to finish a house.

If the teacher decides on all the above, you have a house that you're not satisfied with. You don't use the things that were put in the house for you, so you throw them away.

Then you're left with an empty house, feeling frustrated.

In an ideal world, 100% of the language that a teacher teaches you should be relevant.

100%.

DON'T SETTLE FOR LESS.

Let me tell you a secret. Out of the thousands of English learners I have met in all my career, the ones that make the most progress are the ones that don't attend English class. The ones that make the most progress are the ones that have taken control of their English learning.

This is what I teach now. I teach people how to be one of those English learners.

It's not that teachers and classes are bad. They aren't. What's bad is depending on teachers and classes in order to learn.

Classes can be - and should be - very powerful learning environments.

Often, the problem is that English learners find it difficult to communicate exactly what it is that they want and need.

Why?

Because people are not very good at looking inside their own heads to see what they know and what they don't know. They find it difficult to see what language they need to learn. And they don't know what their strengths and weaknesses are.

> **THIS IS WHAT WE NEED TO TEACH ENGLISH LEARNERS TO DO.**

So let's say you look inside your head, and you determine what you know and what you need.

Maybe you'd then tell the teacher, "I want to learn more vocabulary."

And the teacher would go and find some vocabulary lessons and do gap-fill exercises, match the sentence halves, blah blah blah…

And we're back to the same problem of material irrelevance.

I was once teaching an advanced class, following a student's book. In the book was a two-hour class on bird vocabulary. Yes, bird vocabulary. Can you imagine that?

Useful? If you're an ornithologist, maybe. I didn't have any ornithologists in the class so, naturally, covering that vocabulary was a complete waste of time.

Even if I had had any ornithologists in the class, it would've still been useless. Here's why:

"Hi Maria, my ornithologist student! Today, we're looking at bird vocabulary."

"I already know this vocabulary. I'm an ornithologist."

Introduction

"Oh...erm...well, let's study verbs describing animal noises instead."

So you can see that you really don't need a teacher to learn vocabulary. In fact, you'll learn far more vocabulary without a teacher. And yes, there is a lesson on verbs describing animal noises, and no, I don't recommend it.

In an ideal world, the original conversation between teacher and learner should have gone something like this:

"I want to learn more vocabulary."

"Great! What kind of vocabulary?"

"Oh… I've never really thought about it."

"Well, are there any situations in which you feel that you don't know the necessary vocabulary to have a conversation that flows naturally?"

"Well, yes. I like football, but I have difficulty speaking about it in English because I don't know many of the words related to the sport."

"Fantastic! Go and look for those words in a dictionary and practise them. You don't need me."

If you know what you're missing, you simply need to go and find it, then practise it.

Often, learners don't know what they want or need so they go to class feeling a bit lost, hoping that the teacher will give them some direction, as if the teacher magically knew what the learner needs.

This doesn't often happen and as a result, the language that is taught to them becomes lost too.

It's like looking for something that you've lost, but you don't know what you have lost.

When you can identify *what* you need to learn, the first problem disappears and you can start making progress again.

THE PROBLEM WITH HOW YOU LEARN

*"Everyone has taught you what to learn.
Nobody has taught you how to learn."*

There are nearly 8 billion people on Earth.

That's nearly 8 billion that can speak a language.

More than half of those can speak at least two languages.

That means that it's more common for humans to speak more than one language than just one. The ability to speak more than one language is normal and natural for the brain.

WHAT IS LANGUAGE FOR EXACTLY?

Language is for communication. It's for sharing ideas and communicating our emotions. With language, we can pass on these ideas and emotions through generations and time.

The reason human language is so complex is that as humans, we are social animals. In fact, we are the most social animals on this entire planet.

And because of that, we need a complex language to communicate our complex ideas, thoughts and emotions.

Speaking a language is the most normal thing for the human brain to do.

The human brain is hardwired to learn and speak languages. And not just one language, multiple languages.

If that is true, why do many English learners not make the progress that they want and deserve?

To answer this question, we have to go back to the beginning. Back to when you first started learning English.

Introduction

WHEN DO MOST ENGLISH LEARNERS FIRST HAVE CONTACT WITH ENGLISH?

Most English learners first have contact with the language in school. This was probably the case for you.

In school, an English teacher teaches you English.

At a very early age, you learn that to improve your English, somebody needs to teach it to you.

But when you learn English in school, you don't make much progress, when you consider how many years you spend in English classes in school.

So you start to think that learning another language is difficult and complicated. But you forget that it is the most natural thing for humans to do.

You think that to learn English, somebody must teach it to you. As a result, you start to depend on teachers in order to learn.

If you depend on English teachers to make progress in English, you often become very frustrated.

When you depend on English teachers and classes to improve, your progress is 100% dependent on teachers and classes.

This means that when you attend English classes, you make progress. And when you don't attend classes, you don't make progress. Then, when you stop attending English classes, you start to lose your level.

That's when English learners start to experience the learner frustrations I explained before.

If you depend on English classes to improve, you will always have to attend classes to avoid losing your English.

For the rest of your life.

DO YOU WANT TO HAVE ENGLISH CLASSES FOR THE REST OF YOUR LIFE?

No, of course you don't.

The problem is that everybody teaches you *what to* learn, but nobody teaches you *how to* learn. When you learn *how to* learn, you never need to worry about *what* you learn.

What you need to do is use the natural skill that every human on this planet has: the ability to learn and speak multiple languages.

When you do this, all your progress depends on you.

When you learn *how to* learn, you don't need to depend on anybody else to make progress. You have complete control over your learning.

And that's the key.

When you have complete control over your learning, the problems I've covered simply disappear.

The learning material becomes 100% relevant because *you* decide what you learn.

You enjoy the learning process because *you* decide what you learn and how you learn.

You also have the luxury of deciding not only how you learn, but when you learn and how long you learn for. You will also work towards *your* goals, on *your* time.

This is how to always make progress and never become frustrated.

Introduction

ARE YOU READY TO TAKE CONTROL OF YOUR ENGLISH LEARNING?

"Humans are most motivated when they feel they control their own destiny, and least motivated when they feel that others decide their destiny for them."

In the first three chapters, we covered the main problems with depending on classes to learn English.

We learned that if you continue to do what you've always done, you will continue to be frustrated with your progress in English.

Now comes the question, are you ready to take control of your English learning?

The reality is, learning English is very simple.

If you have good quality contact with English and practise consistently, you will make good progress.

If that is the case, why do many English learners not make the progress that they want and deserve?

For five reasons:

1. **They don't know what good quality contact with English is.**

    They know they need to do something to improve their English, but they don't know what to do.

    They don't know how to practise fluency so that they can speak better and more confidently. As a result, they don't speak. Then they feel bad that they can't speak.

    Maybe you know you need to practise, but you don't know exactly what to do.

    I will teach you the fundamental basics of mastering English on your own, and how to easily find time to practise.

2. **They are not consistent. They have no habit.**

    Maybe you have good intentions and want to practise, but you make excuses or you don't enjoy practising English.

    I will teach you how to be motivated to learn English, how to create a habit, how to improve self-discipline, and how to enjoy the process.

3. **They don't know *what* to learn in English.**

    Most English learners depend on a teacher to teach them the language. However, we have seen that the result of this is that they learn things that aren't relevant to them. They also don't learn from their mistakes, so they always make the same mistakes, over and over again.

    I will teach you how to identify relevant language to learn, how to avoid making mistakes, and how to learn from your mistakes.

    I will also show you how to identify your strengths so you can improve your weaknesses.

4. **They don't know *how* to learn English.**

    The important thing is not what you learn, but how you learn.

    I will show you how to master the most important aspects of English on your own: speaking, listening, pronunciation, grammar and vocabulary. That way, you will know what you need to learn and how you can best learn it.

    I'm not going to teach you what to learn. In fact, I'm not going to teach you any English at all. There are a million other books that will teach you that. Everybody teaches you what to learn in English.

    I'm not going to do that.

    I'm going to teach you how to learn. I'm going to teach you how to take control of your English, and how to master the language on your own.

    I will give you all the tools you need to do this.

Introduction

5. They don't know how to plan and control their English learning.

Creating a practice plan is the final piece of the puzzle. When you know everything else, the only thing you need to do is follow a plan to make sure you are always making progress and you can continue to make progress when you finish this book.

In each chapter, I will give you a solution to a specific problem in English learning. Each problem is an obstacle. Each solution removes an obstacle.

If you eliminate the obstacles in your way, there is nothing stopping you from making the progress you want and deserve.

The main goal of this book is to give you the skills you need to become an independent learner, to never be frustrated, and to create the habit that you will need to master English.

Here are some questions you may have in your head about this book.

"What will I need to do every day?"

On each of the following thirty-one days, you will need to do a few things. First of all, you need to read one chapter of the book. Each chapter has a main topic and then a practice exercise related to the topic.

You will also need to do a speaking exercise and/or listening practice.

At the end of each chapter, there is a very short review section. In the review, I ask you simple questions about the chapter you have just read. The idea is to get you thinking about the content of each chapter and to change the way you think about learning English.

Ideally, you should answer these questions at the end of your day, while you review what you have learned and practised during the day. Answer each question in your own words and think about your answer carefully.

"How many chapters should I read per day?"

There are thirty-one chapters in this book. One for each day of the month that you need to create a new habit.

Read a maximum of one chapter per day. No more.

This is very important as each day you will learn something new and then practise it. Over the next month, you will completely change the way you look at English learning. It's important to absorb this new information slowly in order to understand it well.

It's important to stay with the programme for thirty-one days to create the habit you need to master English.

"What should I do if I miss a day?"

Sometimes, life gets in the way. That's OK. Things happen that are out of your control. If you miss a day, don't feel bad.

Do everything you can to read again the following day. Missing one day isn't a problem; missing two is when it becomes a problem.

If you miss a day, it will normally be because of things that are out of your control. To avoid external distractions, try to read at a time when there is less probability of you being disturbed.

The book is designed to be read in thirty-one days. But sometimes you may not be able to read a full chapter. Don't feel bad and don't punish yourself. If you find that you can't read a full chapter every day, read as much as you can and continue reading the next day.

"What should I do if I don't understand a word or phrase?"

There will be words, phrases and grammar structures that you will see for the first time. You don't need to stop to pick up a dictionary every time you don't understand something.

It's more important to read without being disturbed.

Any language that you don't understand, write it down and check it later, after you finish reading. You should only check a word or phrase if you don't understand the sentence at all.

Introduction

You are about to start the process of becoming a master of your own English learning.

DO YOU ACCEPT THE CHALLENGE?

You need to make a conscious decision now. When you make that decision, there is no turning back. Making the decision is one of the most difficult things to do. Most people only have the desire to master English. Unfortunately, a desire is not enough.

You need to *decide* to master English.

When you make the conscious decision to master English once and for all, you have already done what many people will never do.

Everything after that decision is easy.

ARE YOU READY?

Then let's start.

The first thing you need to do on **Day 1** is find time to practise English.

And it's much easier than you think…

PART I

THE FUNDAMENTAL BASICS

"If you consistently apply the fundamental basics, success is inevitable."

DAY 1

HOW TO FIND TIME TO PRACTISE ENGLISH

"You can't create time, but you can choose how to spend the time you have."

I have no time.

I'm really busy.

Extremely busy.

I have two small children and a busy work schedule. When I say I don't have time, I really mean it.

I started my blog, www.how-to-english.com, in 2017. When you have a blog, you have to write. You find time to write or you have no blog. There is no alternative.

But I had no time to write!

Somehow, if I wanted my blog to help English learners, I had to find time to write. Somehow, I had to go from writing zero words per week to a few thousand. Week after week.

If I couldn't do that, I couldn't reach my goal.

But I have two small children! I work all day! I have to go shopping, cook, clean the house! And what about running? I love running and I need time to run too! Not to mention play the guitar, watch my favourite series. I need to relax or I'll go crazy!

Ask any adult and they'll tell you exactly the same as what I said, "I have no time!"

Then I started to really think about it and I realised that it wasn't really true. It was one of those excuses I made just like everybody else.

The reality is that we say "I don't have time" as an excuse for activities that we don't enjoy or we don't normally do.

Let's look at activities that we don't enjoy first.

It's funny because, although we say we don't have time, we always find time to do the things that we want to do. We don't make excuses not to do them.

It's all about priorities. You have a number of actions that you think you need to do in a day. You then prioritise them based on their importance and whether you enjoy them or not. The most important activities and the ones you enjoy doing go to the top of your list, and the least important and the ones you don't enjoy doing go to the bottom of the list.

Do you enjoy practising and learning English, or is it just something you think you should do?

If you don't enjoy English, your priority should be to learn to enjoy it. If you don't enjoy what you learn, you simply will not learn it.

I will show you how to do this in a few days.

Why can't we find time to do the activities that we don't normally do?

The reason is habit.

THE BRAIN LOVES HABITS.

The brain puts a priority on actions that are part of our habits. The brain will choose to do these actions even if they don't benefit us. We do them simply because they are habit.

That means that there are many actions that we do every day that aren't essential and that don't benefit us in any way.

Day 1

A typical example of this is TV. I'm sure you watch TV, probably every day. You probably have a favourite TV programme that you watch regularly. I'm not saying don't watch TV. There's nothing wrong with TV.

But I'm sure there are programmes that you watch that you don't enjoy. If that is the case, why do you watch them?

Habit.

You probably sit there, in front of the TV and say, "This programme is rubbish!"

But you continue to watch it!

Habit.

You rarely turn off the TV and do something else. Your brain wants to continue the habit because it loves habits.

And there are many other things that you do simply because they form part of your habit.

You do them automatically. You do them because it feels normal to do them. You never stop to think about whether they are actually essential or even good for you.

You just do them.

This is the power of habits.

When you start a new habit and you're able to continue it, it quickly becomes routine and you start to enjoy it and find extra time for it.

Why?

Because the brain makes it a habit and the brain loves habits.

PRACTICE

HOW TO FIND TIME

*"You don't need a lot of time to learn English well.
You just need to use your time well."*

What you're going to do for today's practice exercise is sit down with a pen and paper for a few minutes and write down your typical day. Write it down almost minute by minute and see where your time is going exactly.

Write down the time you spend doing an action or activity and also include the time you spend between activities.

The purpose of this exercise is to find two types of time to practise English: focused time and unfocused time.

Focused time is time that requires your full attention. This type of time is for focused practice. When you do focused practice, you can't do anything else at the same time.

Your reading time is an example of focused time.

Unfocused time is time that doesn't require your full attention. The best way to find it is to find a time when you are doing something, but you could also be doing something else, like practising English.

Washing the dishes, driving or walking to work, having a shower, cleaning the house are all examples of unfocused time.

HOW TO FIND FOCUSED TIME

First, give a 3-star rating to each action or activity in the daily routine that you wrote, based on how important each one is.

Three stars means it is very important. These are actions and activities that you can't remove without causing damage or harm to your life.

Two stars means it is quite important. You can probably live without these things but there may be a little sacrifice.

One star means it's not important and you can remove it without causing problems.

Now think about which one-star activities you would like to carry on doing, and which you could replace with English practice for the next month.

By identifying low-priority activities, you can easily find time. Let's look for some more time.

First, write down all the blocks of time during your day when you are doing something.

Now look at each block of time and decide if you need all that time for that action.

For example, your lunch break at work. Do you need one hour for lunch? What if you have fifty minutes instead? If every day is too difficult for you, what about fifty minutes three times a week?

Can you get to work ten minutes earlier and practise a little before you start work? What about the last ten minutes of your work day?

How much time do you spend relaxing in the evening? If it's three hours, what if you relax for two and a half hours instead?

Is there a programme you watch every day that you don't enjoy or don't need to watch?

Can you dedicate three blocks of twenty minutes per day at the weekend to practise?

You don't need to sit down for an hour or two to study English. You need to find blocks of time during the day when you can practise English. Try to find a few blocks of between fifteen and thirty minutes every day.

It's only for the next month. After that, you will know exactly what you will need to do.

FINDING UNFOCUSED TIME

With your daily routine in front of you, you now need to look for unfocused time. Unfocused time is time that you are doing an activity, but that allows you to do another activity, like English practice. These activities are ones that don't require your full attention.

Do you drive, walk or take public transport to work? How long does it take you?

Do you have a shower or bath? How long does it take you?

Do you cook every day? How long does it take you?

How often do you clean the house? How long does it take you?

When do you go shopping? How long does it take you?

Find a few of these times every day. Underline the ones that are easiest for you and use those times for unfocused practice. Unfocused time is very easy to find.

After the exercise, you will see that, almost by magic, a few hours appear in your day. You don't need all that time to practise English.

Just a little.

You should be able to find blocks of different durations of focused and unfocused time. Five minutes here, ten minutes there, half an hour here, and maybe a block or two of one hour.

Find as many blocks of time of different durations as you can. The blocks of five and ten minutes are the most important. Again, you won't need to use all those times for English but you will at least have an idea of when you can practise English.

Keep your routine near you all the time. With a visual written routine with focused and unfocused times, you can easily see when you can do each practice exercise over the next month.

By doing this exercise in 2017, I was able to identify times to write so that I could go from zero words to a few thousand words every week to work on my blog, without making any sacrifices.

See you tomorrow for Day 2, when I will show you how to make English practice automatic and start to create a new habit.

This new habit will make you the master of your own English learning.

REVIEW

- *How much focused time did you find in total?*
- *How much unfocused time did you find in total?*
- *How many one-star activities are you going to replace with English practise for the next month?*

Do you want more practice? You can find an additional activity to practise the strategies from today's chapter in the free workbook. Visit www.how-to-english.com/workbook

DAY 2

HOW TO TAKE CONTROL OF YOUR ENGLISH LEARNING

"Your brain is your best friend and your worst enemy."

You are very lucky. You have an organ inside your skull called the brain that weighs around 1.3 kilos.

Those 1.3 kilos of jelly comprise by far the greatest learning machine on this planet.

Nothing comes even close.

The human brain is built to learn. It loves learning. It wants to learn. And it loves making progress.

When the brain isn't learning or making progress, it becomes bored and frustrated.

All the brain wants to do is learn and make progress.

So all you need to do is keep learning and keep making progress. That is true for English and almost everything else in your life too.

You bought this book because you want to improve your English. There are many books that will teach you English. But you probably bought this book for one of the reasons that I described in the introduction.

You are either not learning as much English as you want to learn or you are not making progress.

You have good intentions and you want to finally make the progress you deserve.

YOU HAVE THE BEST INTENTIONS.

Unfortunately, good intentions are not enough.

The human brain is the master of making excuses. It's the Olympic champion of making excuses.

Think of it like this.

There are two people in your head: Good Intentions and Instant Gratification.

Good Intentions cares about you and wants you to do well and succeed. It cares about your future and your progress.

Instant Gratification cares about the present. It is only interested in the *now*. It doesn't care about your future. It only wants to feel good now.

Every time you need to make a decision about doing something, you have this internal battle of, "I need to practise English… But I don't want to… Yes, but I really need to practise… But I don't feel like it… But I need to do it now… Let's do it later instead…"

This is a battle between Good Intentions and Instant Gratification.

Good Intentions knows that if you practise English, it will be good for you and your future.

Instant Gratification wants to feel good now. Sitting on the sofa doing nothing feels good *now*. It might not feel good later but Instant Gratification is only interested in the present moment.

Who wins this battle?

The one that fights the hardest or smartest.

Good Intentions is good, but it's not good at fighting.

Instant Gratification is very strong and it nearly always wins the battle.

But fighting is stupid.

Day 2

Fighting is even more stupid when the person you're fighting is yourself.

HOW DO YOU MAKE GOOD INTENTIONS WIN THIS BATTLE?

Because Good Intentions is not good at fighting, the best way is to avoid the battle altogether.

You need to prevent the internal battle from happening.

Practising English is easy. What's difficult is making the decision to practise English at a particular moment.

The brain doesn't like making decisions. When you put the brain in a position where it needs to make a decision, you have this internal battle and the result is that Instant Gratification nearly always wins.

Remove the need to make decisions to practise English and you remove the need to have this internal battle.

How can you do this?

Easy.

You create a system. You create a plan.

An English practice plan.

Yesterday we looked at how to find time. Now you have a good idea of times during the day and week that you can use to practise English.

That's an important step and something that most English learners never do.

Now you need to take those times and do something with them.

Take those times that you found to practise English and write them in your diary as empty blocks. If you don't have a diary, buy one now. You will have lots of blocks of five minutes, ten minutes, maybe half an hour here and there, and hopefully at least one block of one hour in the week. Those blocks of time will be filled with English practice.

The next step in taking control of your English learning is to have control over the decision-making process.

I created a learning system to do this called **PPRR**.

> **PLAN, PRACTISE, REVIEW, REWARD.**

When you implement this learning system, you become unstoppable.

Day 2

PRACTICE

HOW TO PPRR

"Extraordinary results require an extraordinary system."

PLAN

First, you're going to plan the week. You decide **what** you're going to do, **when** you're going to do it and **how long** you're going to do it for.

Take a little time one day per week as your planning time. This is the time when you make all the decisions for the following week related to English practice.

My planning time is Sunday afternoon. This is the perfect time for me because the weekend is nearly over and I can easily focus on the following week. It takes no more than ten minutes.

Choose a time that works best for you. Maybe it's Sunday, maybe it's Monday morning. Whenever. Just make sure that it's the same time every week.

Write down each practice exercise that you will do over the next week. Write them in your diary and specify **what**, **when** and **how long**. For now, you don't need to write anything in those blocks. You only need to have a visual plan of your week with empty blocks. You will start filling those blocks over the next few days.

When you plan your week and make all the decisions once, you remove the need to make decisions about practising and learning English. That way, you remove the need for the internal battle between Good Intentions and Instant Gratification.

PRACTISE

After you plan the week, all you need to do is open your diary each day, see what you need to do and then just do it.

This is when you practise what you decided you would do.

No decisions, no internal battle.

Practice makes perfect.

Practice makes permanent.

REVIEW

At the end of each day, review your day.

Look at the vocabulary and language you practised and learned. Think about them for a moment. What was useful? What was not so useful? What do you want to practise more? Identify the most useful vocabulary and language and mark them so you can practise them later. What went well? What didn't go so well? What will you do differently tomorrow? Maybe you found a way to practise and learn that you liked. Think about how you can do more of that in the future.

In today's world, we often live life thinking about the future.

With English learning, it's important to take a moment to look at the recent past. Reviewing your day is a great way to do this. By doing this, you will remember much more, you will see your progress and you will be able to identify new and enjoyable ways of learning. Looking at the recent past will tell you how to best move into the future.

It will also get you ready for the next day feeling motivated.

Day 2

REWARD

This is the time to congratulate yourself.

You planned the week, you planned the day and you completed the work you wanted to do.

Well done!

Smile. Give yourself a pat on the back. You deserve it.

After each review at the end of each day, think about what you did well. It only takes two minutes. Think about the fact that everything you did today has helped you improve.

Then do something that you like that isn't related to English.

The brain likes rewards. The brain will only want to repeat an action if it likes the action. When you think about the positive aspects of your English improvement every day, your brain will associate English improvement with positive emotions.

That way, you will want to do it again.

The only thing that matters is doing it again.

Nothing else.

So plan, practise, review and reward.

Your practice plan is the system you will use to be a successful and effective English learning machine. Without a system, you will learn grammar at random, remember vocabulary at random, go round and round in circles and never get anywhere.

Making decisions constantly is what most tires the brain. This is why the brain likes habits so much. It doesn't need to make a decision.

When you create a practice plan, it avoids the need for your brain to make a decision about practising English.

You just do it.

You decide exactly when you practise English.

You are the master of your brain, not Good Intentions and Instant Gratification.

Now you are starting to take control of your English learning.

You have won the battle. Now you need to win the war.

REVIEW

- *What day and time are you going to use as your planning time?*
- *Why does planning make it easier to practise?*
- *Do you ever review what you learn?*
- *How can the review part help you learn?*
- *What simple things can you do to reward yourself?*

Plan

Practise

Review

Reward

Do you want more practice? You can find an additional activity to practise the strategies from today's chapter in the free workbook. Visit www.how-to-english.com/workbook

DAY 3

HOW TO ORGANISE WHAT YOU LEARN

"It's not what you do in class that determines your progress. It's what you do when you're not in class."

We have a storeroom in our house. I'm almost scared to go in there.

Not because there are ghosts in it or anything, but because I have no idea what's in there.

Actually, I have an idea what's in there but I prefer not to think about it: roller skates that I've never used, a huge tent that I've used once, fifty skipping ropes that I've obviously never used (don't ask…) and a million other things I have little intention of using again.

And I don't really want to know what's in there because then I'll feel the need to dedicate a whole weekend to throwing away ninety percent of what's in there.

So I just open the door occasionally with my eyes closed and throw a bag of things into it, then quickly close and lock the door.

You put things in the storeroom that you feel don't deserve to be in the house, but that you don't want to throw away yet. So you say, "I know! I'll put them in the storeroom so I can take them back out when I need them".

Then they stay in there forever.

Or sometimes, you go in there and clean everything up, throw everything away and promise yourself to keep it tidy and more or less empty.

After a month, it's full again.

But storerooms are very useful. They help us organise ourselves.

We organise everything in our lives.

Look at your house. It's organised by rooms, each with its own purpose. Kitchen for cooking, living room for relaxation, bedroom for sleeping and the storeroom for stuff you feel bad about throwing away.

The things inside each room are also organised. We keep items in places depending on how easily you want to access them. The items which you use often are put in a location which is easy to get to. The items which you use less often are put in a place which is more difficult to access.

> **EVERYTHING HAS ITS PLACE.**

So what about the information in your own head? How is that organised exactly?

"Erm…what do you mean, Adam?"

Well, how exactly do you organise new information in your head when you learn it?

Many people don't have any method at all for organising what they learn.

We have lists of various kinds (to-do lists, shopping lists, wish lists, etc.) to help us organise our priorities and future actions.

And they're very useful.

However, we normally focus our attention on organising future tasks in our heads, and when we achieve these things, we cross them off our list and they cease to exist.

We don't often have lists or notes for past actions and thoughts, things we've learned in the past.

Day 3

When you're learning English, if you don't organise new language that goes into your head, it gets lost or put in the wrong place.

Just like the items you keep in your house, the objects that you use most frequently are easy to access, and the objects that you use less frequently are more difficult to access.

Imagine you get a new item for your house, and instead of keeping it in the relevant room and drawer, you just throw it into any room and drawer. You'll probably have trouble finding that item in the future.

Likewise, if you learn something but you don't practise it regularly, this information will become more difficult to access.

This is why it's important to organise everything you learn. You will learn more, remember more and your head will be nice and tidy.

Not like my storeroom.

Also, if it's all in one physical place, you can practise it easily. That way, it's always fresh in your mind, and you can easily access it when you need to use it.

The best way to do this is simply by writing everything down. You can see where I'm going with this…

Get a notebook. A notebook just for English.

You need to write down everything you learn.

What is important is to write down only the vocabulary and language that you've learned and key points. Anything that you didn't know a moment ago, but do now, is what you need to write down.

This is key.

Something very interesting happens in the brain when it receives information.

The brain treats all new information equally. This means that it treats important information in the same way as it treats unimportant information. As the information comes in, it doesn't know what is important and not important, so it remembers everything.

For a while…

After a while, it will start to forget everything equally.

It's no good thinking, "Oh, that was important. I'll remember that".

Your brain treats all information equally and will forget important and unimportant information equally.

Unless you do something about it.

Day 3

PRACTICE

HOW TO TAKE NOTES

"A well-organised notebook is a well-organised head."

Get a notebook and start writing everything down that you learn.

You want a notebook only for English notes.

Get a nice book, it will be your companion in English.

You can choose to organise it however you want: by date, skills, categories (expressions, general vocabulary, idioms, etc.) or a long list.

You can use tables, boxes, coloured pens, highlighters or just a pencil.

Whatever floats your boat.

I'm a pencil and categorised notes kind of guy, but that's just me.

What's great is that whichever method you choose to use will be the right method for you, because it will generally reflect how your brain likes to organise information.

If you attend English classes and receive handouts, books or other material, put a priority on your notebook. If you're taking down notes correctly, you will be able to throw away all other teaching material after each class, and only keep your notebook.

After all, everything that's important is in your notebook.

EVERYTHING ELSE IS IRRELEVANT.

Don't worry about having to carry your notebook everywhere with you. If you're out and about and see, hear or read something new in English, write it down in your mobile phone notes (the one object that we always carry around) and copy it into your notebook when you get home.

Then comes the last and most important part: keeping it fresh.

You want to read your notes on a regular basis.

Find a block of ten minutes once or twice a week from your English practice plan and have that focused time to read your notes. Remember, try not to memorise the information, just read it.

Then you should take a couple of minutes to practise any language that isn't completely clear to you. Make practice sentences with the words or grammar that you have difficulty with.

Lastly, take a minute or two to remove any vocabulary that you don't use or don't think you will use. Don't be afraid to do this. You should only practise vocabulary that you want to use or think you will use.

If you take good notes and practise them, you'll remember most of what you learn. If you don't, you'll forget most of what you learn.

You choose.

When you decide what goes into your head, how it goes in and how you use it, you have complete control over your knowledge. As the Chinese proverb goes, "He who controls the front door, controls the house".

REVIEW

- *How do you like to organise new information?*
- *How can taking notes help you practise and remember English?*
- *Do you have problems remembering new information?*
- *When are you going to practise and review your notes every week?*

> Do you want more practice? You can find an additional activity to practise the strategies from today's chapter in the free workbook. Visit www.how-to-english.com/workbook

DAY 4

HOW TO IMPROVE FLUENCY

"If you don't practise playing the piano, you'll never be able to play the piano. If you don't practise speaking, you'll never be able to speak."

When I first met my wife Esther in England, I asked her to speak to me in Spanish.

I knew the very basics of Spanish because I had travelled to South America a few years earlier and had learned some words and expressions.

Not much though.

I couldn't have a conversation in Spanish.

I was interested in languages and I wanted to learn hers, so she started speaking to me in Spanish sometimes, and translating words and expressions from English into Spanish.

After a year, we decided to move to Madrid, Spain. The great thing about teaching English is that you can find work almost anywhere in the world.

My wife had been speaking to me in Spanish for almost a year so I could understand almost everything that people were saying.

But there was a big problem.

I couldn't speak.

I had learned a lot of Spanish but I couldn't say what I knew with my mouth. I had never spoken, so I couldn't speak.

I realised this when I met Esther's family for the first time for dinner.

Everybody was speaking and it was clear to them that I understood most of what they were saying. But I didn't say a word.

"Why isn't Adam saying anything?", my father-in-law asked. Esther explained that I understood Spanish but I couldn't speak, which probably sounded a little strange to him.

It was very frustrating.

This is a similar feeling that many English learners have. They understand a lot when they read or listen to English, but when they need to speak, that's when the problems appear.

Why do many English learners have problems speaking?

For two reasons.

First, they spend most of their time practising listening. They watch films, series and maybe listen to the radio. It's much easier to practise listening because you can do it passively.

Most listening practice is unfocused practice.

You can be lying on the sofa eating popcorn and chocolate, watching your favourite TV series and you'll be practising your listening skills.

With most listening practice, you don't actually *do* anything.

With speaking, it's the opposite. To practise speaking you have to *do* something.

You have to think about what you want to say, think about how you'll say it, then produce sounds using the muscles in your mouth.

It's not much, but it's more effort than doing nothing.

So most of the time, people choose to practise listening instead of speaking. As a result, their listening improves but they can't speak comfortably.

Then they have a big problem.

Day 4

Most English learners need to improve their speaking skills. But most people don't because of the second reason.

Most people think that improving their speaking skills is difficult. They say they can't practise speaking because they don't know any native English speakers, or they don't have time to get a teacher or go to classes, or they live too far away from language exchanges.

These are not good reasons not to practise speaking.

Here's an easy question for you. What do you need to do to improve your speaking skills?

SPEAK.

And to practise speaking in English, all you need to do is speak in English. What I'm saying is that you don't need a person in front of you to practice speaking English.

Just speak on your own.

I know what you're thinking. Every time I say this, everybody disagrees with me. They say things like, "But who's going to correct me?"

Think about this. What do you think the perfect situation is to practise speaking English?

Most people say something like speaking to a native English speaker in their country.

OK. So imagine you're having a conversation with that person and you make a mistake. Do you think that person will correct you?

No. Of course not.

Nobody is going to correct you.

In a conversation, you practise two skills: speaking and listening.

If you remove the person you're speaking to, what skill are you practising now?

Exactly. Speaking.

The only difference between speaking to another person and speaking on your own is that you don't practise listening. Well, you're only interested in practising speaking so it doesn't matter. In fact, speaking on your own is actually better than speaking to another person if you want to improve fluency.

Why?

First of all, you can choose what you talk about. In a conversation, you have to consider the other person. Secondly, you can listen more carefully to what you are saying, experiment with language, and repeat what you are saying as many times as you want. You can't do any of this in a conversation. Lastly, you can speak more because you don't have to wait for the other person to speak. Five minutes speaking on your own is like a fifteen-minute conversation with another person.

> **SPEAKING IS THE ONLY WAY TO IMPROVE YOUR FLUENCY IN ENGLISH.**

What is fluency exactly?

Fluency describes how easy it is for you to produce the English that you know.

The great thing about fluency is that it is level-independent. I have taught A2 students with excellent fluency, and I have also taught C2 students with very bad fluency.

C2 students with bad fluency have great results on paper but they can't hold a conversation comfortably.

Fluency is the connection between your brain and your mouth. When you speak in English, you make this connection stronger. When the connection is strong, you find it easy to speak in English.

Day 4

When you have problems with fluency, you have the feeling that your brain is going faster than your mouth.

Your brain knows what to say, but you can't find the right word in English. When you find the correct word, you can't say it correctly.

When you practise speaking English, what you're doing is making it easier to find the correct word in your head, and then making it easier to actually say the word.

THAT'S HOW YOU IMPROVE FLUENCY.

And you don't need a person in front of you to do it.

When you practise speaking English, you strengthen connections in the brain. Remember, connections aren't permanent. The connections are there if you use them. If you don't use them, you lose them.

Fluency is different from all the other skills in English. It's very easy to improve and you see results very quickly.

But that also means that it's very easy to lose. If you don't practise for a few days, you lose everything.

I compare fluency to juggling. To juggle, you can start throwing and catching the balls in sequence quite quickly. You don't need a lot of effort to keep the balls moving and you don't need to concentrate very much either.

What is very important, though, is to keep the balls moving. If you don't throw or catch one ball, they all fall to the floor.

Keep the balls moving.

Speak every day.

You don't need to speak a lot. You don't need to speak with a lot of effort. But you must speak every day.

I will show you how to do this.

PRACTICE

HOW TO IMPROVE FLUENCY THE EASY WAY

"It's the small changes in habits that give the best results."

This is my favourite speaking exercise.

It's so easy that you'll find it difficult to make an excuse not to do it.

You take some text in English, and you read it out loud.

What makes it a great speaking exercise is that it practises the physicality of producing English words and sounds. It strengthens the connection between brain and mouth.

If you do this exercise regularly, the words will start to flow easily.

You'll notice two things when you do this exercise: you'll feel tired afterwards and you'll remember little or nothing of the text you just read.

It's tiring because as you read, the brain receives the information through the eyes, then you say it immediately using your mouth.

It's tiring because the brain has to work extra.

Any practice exercise that makes you feel tired afterwards is a good indication that it's an effective exercise.

You'll remember little or nothing of the text for the same reason. The words enter through the eyes and leave through the mouth at the same time.

When you read out loud, your brain doesn't process the information. It's not a reading exercise, it's a speaking exercise.

The idea isn't to read and understand the text. The idea is to say the

Day 4

words and sentences that are in the text.

There are two ways to do this exercise and each one practises a different aspect of speech.

The first is to read out loud slowly and carefully. If you are reading dialogue in fiction, try to say the words in the same way that the character would say them. Use intonation, sentence stress and pauses when necessary. By practising these parts of speech, you will start to use them when you speak and you will sound much more natural. You will be easier to understand and your speech will have more impact.

The other way is to speed-read the text out loud. Try to read as quickly as possible, being careful to pronounce the words correctly, of course. Repeat the paragraph a few times, concentrating on sounds and words that you have problems with. Reading quickly is great for strengthening the connection between the brain and the mouth and will make it easier for you to speak naturally and as quickly as you want.

Your practice exercise for today is to read the first two pages of this chapter out loud.

First, read it slowly and carefully, paying attention to intonation, sentence and pauses.

After, speed-read the same first two pages.

If there is a word that you don't know how to pronounce, put that word into an online dictionary and click the play button to hear how it is pronounced.

Tomorrow, I will show you three more speaking exercises to do that take no more than five minutes. You will see that after a week, you will feel much more comfortable and confident speaking English.

REVIEW

- *Do you find it difficult to speak in English?*
- *How often do you usually speak in English?*
- *How much time do you spend listening to English compared to speaking?*

Plan

Practise

Review

Reward

> Do you want more practice? You can find an additional activity to practise the strategies from today's chapter in the free workbook. Visit www.how-to-english.com/workbook

DAY 5

HOW TO MASTER FLUENCY

"There should be a filter between your brain and your mouth."

Yesterday you did your first speaking exercise to improve fluency.

How did it go? Did it feel strange while you were doing it? How did you feel afterwards?

Speaking out loud on your own can feel strange the first few times you do it. That's because when you speak in a normal conversation, you don't usually listen to yourself.

When you speak on your own, you start to listen to yourself. It can feel strange in the beginning and that's normal, but that's actually great. When you start listening to what you say when you speak, you begin to hear things that you never normally hear. Suddenly, you start hearing mistakes that you regularly make, problems with pronunciation, intonation and lots of other parts of speech that you can start to correct and perfect. You start to become more self-aware.

Self-awareness is a powerful learning tool.

You will start to analyse the words you use, your pronunciation, your grammar, and you will start to think about your choice of words and language.

You had probably never done this until now.

The small changes in the way you look at language will totally change the way you learn English.

Today, I will give you three more speaking practice exercises which, along with reading out loud, are the absolute best exercises to master speaking and fluency.

There are lots of different things you can do to practise speaking: get a teacher, go to a language exchange, move to an English-speaking country or marry an English speaker (my wife did this one and she's seen great results).

You already know these. The obvious problem with many of these is that they are not very accessible or easy to do. They require extra effort and time, and I know how difficult it is to find extra time.

I'm not going to tell you about those. I'm more interested in teaching you easy and effective tips and tricks to improve fluency in English with as little effort as possible, very little time and with great results.

The best thing about these speaking exercises is that you can do them anywhere. In the shower, in the car, walking to work or any other unfocused time in your practice plan.

Each of the following speaking exercises has an emphasis on one aspect of English. There's one for vocabulary, one for grammar and another for typical phrases.

Together, they cover all the language you need to communicate well.

Let's look at the first one.

GENERAL OBSERVATION

In this speaking exercise, all you need to do is talk about the world around you.

Talk about the people and objects you can see, what they are doing, why you think they are doing those actions. Find adjectives related to the objects and adverbs related to the actions.

Describe what you can see in as much detail as possible. You may find

Day 5

it difficult in the beginning. It's probably something you have never done before.

The easiest way to do it is as a brainstorming exercise. All you need to do is say as many words as possible as quickly as possible. Name all the objects you can see. Then give an adjective to every object you can see. Then give a verb to every object you can see. Then you will begin to form sentences.

Take this moment right now as an example.

Where are you reading this book right now? In your living room? In bed? At work? On a beach?

Put this book down and say as many nouns as possible from what you can see around you.

After, say each noun with an adjective. Then say where certain objects are in relation to other objects. Then talk about the people you can see. What are they doing? Where are they going?

You can do it while you are watching a film. Imagine you are explaining the scene to a friend over the phone, what would you say?

Use your imagination. The possibilities are limitless.

Now here's the most important part of these exercises.

Every time you want to say something but you don't know how, write it down on a piece of paper or in your mobile notes and look it up in a dictionary later.

Some of the best vocabulary that you can learn are words and phrases that you want to say, but you don't know how.

As you do these speaking exercises, think about the words and language that you are saying and ask yourself if you think they are correct or not.

For example, maybe you are talking about what you can see in your living room and you say, *"There is a clock in the wall...on the wall...is it in the wall or on the wall?"*

Write it down and check later (by the way, it's **on** the wall).

Over time, the sentences you say will become more and more complex, and you will find it easier to talk about the world around you.

The words will start to flow more easily, and you will be able to form sentences more quickly.

Speaking in English will feel easier.

You will become more fluent.

It's a fantastic exercise in observation. It allows you to see the world around you and to be present for a moment. It's very relaxing and you will learn and practise a lot of vocabulary.

RUNNING COMMENTARY

This speaking exercise is great for practising grammar.

In a running commentary, you will speak non-stop for five minutes about the subject of your choice. When you speak, you will use full sentences in a variety of tenses.

To do this, you need to talk about the past, the present and the future. All you need is a topic to talk about.

An easy example is to talk about what you did this morning, what you're doing now and what you're going to do later.

Here's an example.

"Right now I'm doing the washing up because I've just finished lunch. I was really hungry because I went for a long run in the park this morning. I had more free time than usual so I ran further than I normally do. When I finish the washing up, I will start writing. I want to finish the chapter I'm writing before I pick up my children from school..."

And so on…

It doesn't matter what you talk about and it doesn't matter what you say.

Just talk.

Your mind is always saying something. All you need to do is say it out loud.

Again, think carefully about what you're saying and ask yourself if the grammar and vocabulary are correct.

If you're not sure, write it down and check later.

You can talk about last weekend and next weekend. You can talk about your day at work or a presentation you are going to give tomorrow. It could be about your last holiday and where you plan to go for your next holiday.

It doesn't matter. Just make sure you talk about the past, the present and the future.

IMAGINARY CONVERSATION

I'm sure you already have a good idea of what you need to do for this exercise.

That's right. You have an imaginary conversation with someone.

Who?

You decide.

It could be your best friend, your boss or a meeting you're going to have at work. It could be a particular situation that you have difficulties in like ordering in a restaurant, checking in at an airport or hotel, introducing yourself or visiting a business client.

You can speak just as yourself or you can speak as both people in the conversation.

Whatever feels best for you.

When I do this exercise to practise my Spanish I often have an imaginary conversation with my friend Jorge. It's easy because he's my friend so I know what he will say. Or, I choose a typical situation that I have problems with to identify relevant language to learn.

The purpose of this speaking exercise is to identify typical phrases that we use in spoken English and conversations.

Again, every time you want to say something but you don't know how, write it down and look it up later.

THE HOW TO COMMUNITY

Even better than an imaginary conversation. Here, you can actually speak to real people and make massive improvements in your fluency.

In *The How To Community* - my private community of independent English learners - you get unlimited speaking and fluency practice with the other members. It is a great way to speak every day and meet other English learners from all over the world.

Go to the end of this book to find out what else you can get by joining.

Day 5

PRACTICE

HOW TO SPEAK EVERY DAY

"Think before you speak."

Do one of these speaking exercises today.

Put the other two into your practice plan and do them over the next two days. See which ones you like best and which ones give you the best results.

When you have done all of the fluency practice exercises, add them all to your practice plan over the next week. You need to have at least one fluency exercise every day in your practice plan.

Experiment with different topics to speak about. If you have difficulties thinking of a topic to talk about, you can start by using the questions in the review section at the end of each chapter. All you need to do is answer each question out loud and justify your answer. And remember, you must say everything out loud.

These speaking exercises are some of the best unfocused practice you can do. Fluency practice doesn't require a lot of time or effort, and you will see the results very quickly.

The purpose of speaking practice is to improve fluency and identify relevant language to learn and practise.

The language you learn from doing these exercises is the most relevant language you can learn because it's something you want to say but you don't know how.

You can also do these exercises almost anywhere, even in front of other people. You can do speaking practice in the supermarket for example. All you need to do to avoid people thinking you are crazy is put your mobile phone to the side of your head.

Everyone will think you are having a real conversation.

It's radical, yes. But it works.

You have no excuse.

Fluency practice should be the most regular practice that you do. You need to practise fluency every day and, ideally, two or three times a day.

If you miss a day, it's not a disaster. Just make sure you do it again the day after.

Missing one day is not a problem. Missing two is when the problems begin.

Do you remember how I compared fluency to juggling? You get fluency quickly but if you aren't consistent, you lose it quickly too.

Be consistent.

Five minutes, three times a day will make a massive difference and after a week, you will start speaking much more comfortably and confidently.

After six months, you'll be a speaking machine.

Day 5

REVIEW

- *In what situation are you going to do the running commentary?*
- *What past, present and future situations are you going to speak about?*
- *Who are you going to have an imaginary conversation with?*
- *What unfocused time is best for you to practice fluency?*
- *In what situations do you have most problems speaking English?*

Plan

Practise

Review

Reward

Do you want more practice? You can find an additional activity to practise the strategies from today's chapter in the free workbook. Visit www.how-to-english.com/workbook

DAY 6

HOW TO MASTER LISTENING FOR SPECIFIC INFORMATION

THE ABSOLUTE BEST LISTENING EXERCISE YOU CAN DO

"We can all hear perfectly, but we are very bad listeners."

A student arrived in my class a few winters ago with a horrible cold. Pale skin, bloodshot eyes and blocked nose.

He looked and sounded horrible.

I asked him if he was alright, and he said he was just a little ill.

"Get well soon!", I said.

"Thanks", he replied.

As soon as he thanked me, I asked him to repeat what I had just said to him. He paused for a moment before eventually saying, "Erm, I don't know. Well, I know what you said, but I don't know how you said it".

He said it in Spanish (*que te mejores*) to show that he understood the sentence, but he could not say the exact words I had used. Not one word. Even though he understood me perfectly.

I do this with my students all the time. When I see that they understand a sentence that I say, I ask them to repeat it word for word.

Nine times out of ten, they can't.

It's a little bit cruel, but it demonstrates a very important point.

Humans are really bad listeners. We have very selective hearing.

THE HUMAN BRAIN HEARS WHAT IT WANTS TO HEAR.

Once I spent a whole two hours calling one of my students David. It wouldn't have been a problem, except that his name was actually Javier.

I realised near the end of the class, and apologised saying, "Sorry Javier, I've been calling you David for the last two hours!"

"Really? I didn't realise", he replied.

Two hours calling him by a different name, and he didn't even hear it.

You may be able to hear well, but that doesn't mean you can listen well.

Why is this exactly?

In face-to-face conversation, the words that you use aren't that important.

Most of what you understand when a person is speaking to you, you get from the context, eye contact, intonation, body language, and word and sentence stress.

You can see this when you are in a country trying to communicate, but you don't know the language.

What do you do? You exaggerate all of these things.

And often, you are actually able to communicate.

These things are the true international language that everybody understands. You can see that words are not that important in everyday communication.

But, when you're learning a language, words are very important. If you don't hear the words, you cannot learn them.

So why does the brain prioritise these things over words?

The answer is in energy consumption.

The human brain represents just 2% of total body weight.

That's pretty small.

But it consumes 20% of all the energy used in the body and uses 25% of the body's oxygen.

That's one very hungry little organ.

As with anything that uses a lot of energy, efficiency is a top priority. And so, the brain is obsessed with saving energy. It tries to use as little energy as possible.

How can the brain save energy in a conversation?

By listening to less, by processing fewer words, and by using more energy-efficient processes.

Observing body language, listening to intonation, and understanding the context require far less energy than listening to and processing every word you hear.

So the brain puts more importance on those things and listens to less.

So it listens to the subject and object, the verbs, the nouns, the adjectives, and not much else.

This is all that is needed to understand what the person is talking about.

The brain doesn't process most verb tenses, prepositions, many adverbs, auxiliary verbs, and all the other smaller details of the language.

It is precisely this kind of language that English learners make the most mistakes with!

> **THE BRAIN LISTENS FOR THE GENERAL UNDERSTANDING AND IGNORES THE SPECIFIC.**

It's important to understand that the brain may hear those words, but it doesn't process them. That means it will forget them very quickly. Almost instantly.

This is the logical thing for the brain to do.

Why work more when you can work less and get the same result?

However, this is a bad thing when you're learning another language. Listening is when you most learn, and if you're only processing half of what you hear, you stop learning from listening.

And then your progress goes flat.

Unfortunately, most listening practice in standard English teaching focuses on practising listening to get the general understanding. And most of the listening practice that learners do on their own is also listening for general understanding.

If you practise listening for general understanding, you will get good at listening for the general understanding.

Nothing more.

Listening in this way will not improve your listening skills. It's not what you practise, it's how you practise. Your brain is already good at listening for general understanding. It's what it does best. You don't need to practise that.

Your brain is not good at listening in detail. So that's what you need to practise if you want to improve your listening.

There's one exercise that puts an end to this problem: dictation.

I could write about dictations all day. They're great.

Dictations force the brain out of its comfort zone and make it listen to and process every word it hears.

When you do dictations in your own language, you're practising spelling. And they're boring. When you do dictations in another language, it's a completely different exercise.

Dictations will completely revolutionise your listening skills.

Day 6

And I say that from experience.

When I was twelve, my family and I moved to France, and I started in a French school.

We used to do dictations at school in French class, but I didn't know the language. My first finished dictations were blank pieces of paper.

A disaster.

Slowly, as my French improved, I started hearing more and more.

After one year, I was getting the best marks in the class in dictation. Better than the French kids in the class.

I am no genius.

I was getting the best marks in the class precisely because it wasn't my first language.

When you do dictations regularly, you start to hear things that most people don't.

Many years later, I became an English teacher.

I started doing dictations with my students and the same thing happened. The first few dictations were very bad. After a few months, my students were writing perfect dictations and they all really enjoyed doing them.

Seriously, if you do dictations three times a week, in six months your life will be completely different.

You'll be much better at English, you'll be more attractive, you'll earn more money...everything will improve.

Well...maybe not everything in your life, but they are really very good.

PRACTICE

HOW TO DO DICTATIONS

"If your aim is to get the general understanding, then that is what you'll get. Nothing more."

I'm sure you can imagine what the practice exercise is for today.

That's right, dictation.

Here's how you do it.

Go to www.ted.com and choose a video that you think you'll find interesting. After you find a video that you want to use for the dictation on TED.com, you need to search for the same video on YouTube (all videos from TED are also available on YouTube).

The reason is that if you use a computer to do the dictation (which I recommend), it's easier to do it on YouTube. It's difficult to use a pen to write and the mouse to control the video at the same time. On YouTube, you don't need to use the mouse to control the video.

After you click on the video, you can just tap the spacebar on your keyboard to pause and the left arrow key to go back five seconds. You can also go back easily using your mobile and the TED app.

Now take one minute of speech from the video. Listen to the first five or ten seconds and write down every word you hear. Repeat those few seconds again and write down anything you missed. You can repeat as many times as you like, it doesn't matter.

Then listen to the following five seconds and write every word you hear.

It's important to write down every word. If you don't hear the word, simply write down what you hear. Write down the sound you hear,

Day 6

and it may help you identify the word later when you check.

After you dictate one minute of dialogue, listen to the whole thing without pausing.

Now you have your written dictation. Next comes the second exercise.

Now you need to look at what you've written, think about what you've written, and analyse the language in the sentences that you've written.

Do the sentences make sense? Are they in the correct tense and do they follow the correct structure? Are the correct prepositions there? Plurals? Are the verbs conjugated correctly?

These are some of the things that you may not have heard, but by looking at what you have written, you can correct mistakes you have made and identify missing words.

When you're done, you need to check what you've written.

To do this, you need to go back to the video on TED.com. Near the video, click on *transcript*. Here, you can see every word the speaker said in the presentation.

Make any corrections in red and save all the dictations you do in chronological order. As you look through them over a few months, you'll see a clear reduction in the amount of red colour in your dictations.

All in all, it takes fifteen minutes.

Another way to do dictations is with your favourite TV series or even films. Find a scene from the series on YouTube and do the dictation as I described above. To check it, you need to find the transcript. Thankfully, you can find transcripts for nearly every series online. Simply search online for the episode name and the word *transcript*, and you will be able to check what you wrote with the transcript.

Find fifteen minutes of focused time in your practice plan to do your dictation either today or tomorrow. Then plan another two dictations over the next six days and write them in your practice plan. Every week, you will need to do three dictations. If you have time and want to do more, that's fine. But three per week is the minimum.

Open up your practice plan, schedule a few dictations over the next week, and look forward to making more progress than you have ever made in your listening skills.

Enjoy!

REVIEW

- *Which speaking practice exercise are you doing today?*
- *What do you find difficult when you listen in English?*
- *Do you find it difficult to listen for detail in English?*
- *What days and times will be best to do your dictations?*

Plan

Practise

Review

Reward

Do you want more practice? You can find an additional activity to practise the strategies from today's chapter in the free workbook. Visit www.how-to-english.com/workbook

DAY 7

HOW TO LEARN BY LISTENING
IT ALL STARTS WITH LISTENING

"If you only do what is easy, the journey will be hard."

My family and I moved to rural France when I was twelve.

I started in a French school in March of 1993 knowing zero French.

That first day of school was by far the most frightening day of my life.

I remember sitting on the steps that went up to the headmaster's office feeling completely petrified, watching all the children in the playground. I couldn't understand what they were saying but I knew they were talking about me and my brother.

They didn't often get new pupils in the school, and much less a couple of English boys, one wearing a Guns 'n Roses T-shirt (me).

It was the kind of fear that's so intense that you look everywhere for somewhere to run, but you realise that there is nowhere to run.

The headmaster introduced us to all the children in the school playground, told them to help us and be patient with us, then my brother and I parted ways and we each went into our respective classrooms.

I knew the children were going to ask me if I could speak French so I had memorised an answer, *"Un peu, mais pas beaucoup"*, which means *"a little, but not much"*.

When Gilles, a boy from my class, asked me if I could speak French, I replied with my prepared answer.

He laughed and said that *a little* is the same as *not much*. And he was right. I felt stupid that I'd chosen that reply.

Everybody laughed.

Then I felt even more stupid.

That was the first sentence I said in French. It was also the last time I spoke in French in school for six months.

I became the quiet English kid in the class.

WHAT DID I DO FOR THE NEXT SIX MONTHS?

I spent that time listening to French, putting the pieces of the language together. During the summer holidays, I met some other kids who didn't go to my school and I started speaking and having conversations.

When I started school again in September, I was basically fluent in French.

Everyone in my class was shocked. The quiet English kid was suddenly a confident, French-speaking teenager. I made friends, became an active member of the class and I could focus on being a teenager, instead of worrying about my French.

Everything changed after that.

And it all started with listening.

Listening is the most important skill in learning a language.

Speaking is the most important skill you need to use the language, but you don't learn by speaking. You learn by listening.

Learn a language by listening.

Practise a language by speaking.

All the foundations of a language are built from simply listening to the language.

If you listen to a language you've never heard for long enough, your brain will slowly put all the pieces together, and you'll eventually start to understand the language.

When you can understand the language, you start to say words and speak.

This is exactly what babies and young children do.

They spend the first year or two of their lives listening to their parents, relatives, the TV, absorbing the language and putting the pieces of the language together.

After a whole year, maybe longer, they say their first word.

Another year of listening and saying individual words goes by until they are finally able to join words and make short sentences.

This is how humans (babies and adults) learn languages.

Listening is innate.

IT ALL STARTS WITH LISTENING.

Good listening skills will make you an extremely effective language learner. But listening is a skill, and like any skill, it must be practised and perfected to get all the benefits from it.

You already know the benefits of listening for specific information and how dictations will take you to the next level in listening.

But what about listening for the general understanding? What is the best way to improve that type of listening?

TV series and films?

Maybe not…

Well, it's not that watching films and series is bad.

It isn't. It's fun, relaxing and entertaining. Just don't only watch TV.

But not because I think you should spend less time in front of the TV. That's none of my business.

It's about the quality and consistency of the contact that you have with English.

Too many people spend too much time only watching films and series in English to improve. Or they go Monday to Friday without any contact with English, then spend the weekend watching lots of TV to compensate.

If you watch TV in English, you get good at watching TV in English. But that doesn't mean you get good at English.

You get good at how you practise, not what you practise.

If you want to really improve, you need to hit English from all angles.

The key here is variety.

Also, if you go a long time without any contact with English, watching a lot of TV over the weekend can't compensate for the five days of no contact.

The key here is consistency.

But the biggest problem with only watching TV in English is that it just isn't a very good listening exercise. It's better for vocabulary than it is for improving your listening.

We know that in a face-to-face conversation, only a small percentage of the message you want to communicate is the words you say. The vast majority is in the form of body language (posture, facial expressions, gestures and so on) and other verbal elements like intonation, sentence and word stress.

Not the words you say.

This also means that most of what you understand when watching TV doesn't come from the words.

Most of what you understand comes from the visuals. You can prove this by watching a programme without any sound. On mute. You'll notice that you can more or less know what's happening without listening to a single word.

That's not exactly a problem in itself because language is all of these things. But if you're trying to improve your listening skills, you can't only watch TV because only a small part of what you practise will be listening.

If you want to practise listening 100%, you need practice that gives you 100% listening.

That means no visuals.

To really improve your listening skills, you need to remove the visuals.

What are the best examples of listening practice without visuals?

1. **Podcasts**

    There are thousands of podcasts in English as they're very popular in the English-speaking world. And they don't even need to be about learning English. Find a podcast in English about your hobbies and interests and start listening.

    You like running? There are running podcasts. You like science? There are podcasts about that too. You like gardening? You get the idea…

    There are also hundreds of podcasts for English learners. I personally recommend a combination of English learning podcasts and podcasts in English related to your hobbies and interests.

2. **Radio**

    There are loads of great radio stations out there.

    Think of all the English-speaking countries in the world. In each country, you can find both national and local radio stations.

    You can search for these online and listen to them live on your way to work or while doing housework.

The fantastic thing about listening to radio stations from all over the world is that you get a local perspective of the news and can hear a variety of accents.

A good place to start is BBC World Service.

The language is slightly adapted for a more international audience and they cover world news from a global perspective.

Alternatively, you can easily find local radio stations and listen to them live.

A search on Wikipedia for *radio stations in Tennessee* gives a list of over one hundred radio stations. You can also see the topic that each radio station specialises in. A quick Google search for the name of a radio station plus the word *live* will take you to the website where you can listen to that radio station live.

You can do this search for any city or country in the world and discover a whole world of English-speaking radio.

It's fun and it becomes very addictive!

3. **Audiobooks**

    This one is the best.

    I doubt many (if any) of you have "read" an audiobook, even in your own language.

    It's a great way to read a novel as you become completely immersed in the story. A book has on average 80,000 words in it. That's 80,000 words that you'll listen to and absorb.

    A good way to start is by listening to an audiobook of a book you've read in your own language. Or if you like a challenge, get one that's on your to-read list.

    Try it. I guarantee you'll love it.

Day 7

CONCLUSION

Listening without visuals is some of the best listening practice you can do.

When you listen without the visuals, you find that you start to create the visuals yourself. It shows how important they are for comprehension. When you create the visuals yourself in your head, it helps you understand and memorise the vocabulary and phrases.

Clever brain.

So continue watching your favourite shows and films in English. All contact with English is better than no contact with English.

Just make sure you also practise listening without the visuals to really make progress in listening.

Listening without visuals is the perfect unfocused practice that you can do almost anywhere.

Choose some unfocused time and start listening without visuals every day. In the car or walking to work, cleaning the house, having a shower, in the supermarket, in the gym…

Make a habit of listening without visuals and eventually, you will do it automatically.

Your listening comprehension will be better than ever after a few weeks.

PRACTICE

HOW TO LEARN VOCABULARY WITH FILMS AND SERIES

"Quality contact + Consistent practice = Progress."

As I explained earlier, watching films and series is better for learning vocabulary than for improving listening.

What kind of vocabulary is it good for?

Interjections, and short phrases and replies.

No way!

Wow, really?

You've got to be kidding!

Are you serious?

Are you pulling my leg?

All these short replies mean that you're surprised and shocked about what the person is telling you.

Maybe you think it's obvious that they mean that, and you're right. But how many of those phrases do you use when you speak?

These are the phrases, interjections and short replies that we native speakers use.

If you want to sound more like a native English speaker, this kind of vocabulary is what will help you achieve that. And series are perfect for practising this kind of language.

Here's how to learn and practise interjections and short replies with series.

Day 7

The best kind of series to watch is comedy, like *Friends* or *Big Bang Theory*, because they use a lot of this kind of vocabulary for emphasis, but you could do this with any other series you are watching in English.

As you watch the series, try to hear every time they use an interjection or short reply.

When you think you hear one, go back a few seconds and listen again.

Then observe the situation and context. Look at the person's body language and their reaction. What emotion is the person expressing with the words they say?

Write it down and practise it later by imagining another situation in which you could use that interjection.

This is some of the best vocabulary you can learn if you want to sound natural and more like a native English speaker.

English learners often think that as they improve their level, they need to learn long and complicated sentences to express themselves.

But native speakers don't use long and complicated sentences when they speak, they use simple sentences with short phrases and interjections.

The better your English, the more you can express with fewer words.

When you can express more with less, that's when your level really improves.

REVIEW

- *What unfocused time are you going to use to listen to the radio, a podcast or an audiobook?*
- *When is your next dictation?*
- *Which speaking practice are you doing today?*
- *Which series are you going to watch to listen for interjections?*

Plan

Practise

Review

Reward

> Do you want more practice? You can find an additional activity to practise the strategies from today's chapter in the free workbook.
> Visit www.how-to-english.com/workbook

DAY 8

MOTIVATION, SELF-DISCIPLINE AND HABITS (PART 1)
HOW TO THINK IN THE LONG TERM

*"When you eat a seed, you give your present self a little food.
When you plant a seed, you give your future self a lot of food."*

Each year, millions if not billions of people make New Year's resolutions.

Of all the resolutions that are made, learning a new language and losing weight by dieting are two of the most common.

Every year, people make the same promise to themselves that they will do one, or the other, or often both.

Many people, unfortunately, fail to achieve either.

Just like a donkey with a carrot hanging in front of its mouth to make it move forward. They feel that the carrot is always just a little bit too far away to bite. But they keep pushing towards their goal, unable to bite that carrot hanging in front of their mouths. Sometimes the carrot almost touches their teeth, but they are never able to bite into it, and the carrot escapes them again.

Then they get frustrated, maybe punish themselves, then give up.

But that damn carrot looks so tasty. They really want that carrot, they need that carrot. So they try again.

And the vicious circle starts all over again.

You know that feeling. We've all felt it with something.

These two goals share something in common.

What do they have in common?

Well, to put it simply, they are both really easy to achieve. I mean, REALLY easy. In theory…

With learning a language, if you practise a little bit every day, then over time you'll improve.

That's it. There's no magic.

With losing weight, if you eat a little bit better, and move your body around a bit through exercise, then over time you'll lose weight.

Done.

Again, no magic.

Then why on earth isn't everybody fluent in another language and slim?

The magic words in the above scenarios are "over time", and humans are really bad at thinking long-term.

We often forget that we are animals. We like to think that we are extremely intelligent beings that are in complete control of our actions. But the reality is that most of our daily actions follow routines and habits that are dictated by primitive chemical reactions.

Our brains are programmed to look for instant rewards.

INSTANT GRATIFICATION

Most habits are formed by an action which is then followed by a reward, in the form of dopamine released in the brain.

If you do something that the brain likes, it will release dopamine (and dopamine feels good…).

Day 8

As humans, and therefore animals, we are always looking for that dopamine reward. We want to feel good.

This dopamine release is nearly always for instant rewards, and hardly ever for a reward that will come later. We have to remember that primal instincts are there to keep us alive and survive another day.

INSTANT SURVIVAL, INSTANT REWARD.

Our ancestors' only priority was to live another day, not worry about events that may happen in six months. Dopamine was the reason those ancestors hunted an animal for hours and hours, killed it, then ate it. The brain released dopamine, they lived another day, and the dopamine motivated them to look for more opportunities to find food.

Dopamine teaches an animal to repeat an action if there is some instant benefit to that action. For example, food.

That is the way a habit is formed. It's been with us for thousands of years. And for good reason.

It's the only way the brain can motivate you to do something. More importantly, it's the only way the brain tells you to repeat an action. If you do something that doesn't deliver an instant reward, then no dopamine.

The result? You don't actively seek to repeat that action.

No habit is formed.

Here's an example. If you eat a piece of cake, the brain detects sugar and fat. Sugar and fat contain lots of calories, which was useful for surviving another day 50,000 years ago. The brain releases dopamine, a habit starts to form, and then you search for more cake.

Very useful 50,000 years ago. Our worst enemy today.

This chemical reaction is so hardwired into the brain and so strong, that it is extremely difficult to fight.

As a result, it makes us really bad at planning for the future. How much money have you saved for your retirement, by the way?

One of the only times we ignored this instant reward system – and saw the benefits of long-term planning – was during the agricultural revolution.

You plough a field, sweat, plant seeds, cover the seeds with earth, water them, and nearly break your back in the process. What's the instant reward?

Nothing.

But, if you cared for the plants that grew from the seeds, and waited a few months, you could enjoy an abundance of food.

This was the first real revolution. It dramatically changed human survival in the long term. We prospered and conquered the world.

This is also one of the aspects of being a human being that makes us so different from other animals. We have the ability to choose.

Most animals function by instinct. If an animal sees some food, it will probably eat it.

When you see a seed, you have a choice. You can decide between eating the seed now, or planting that seed to get more seeds in the future.

Acting in the short term may help us survive today, but long-term planning is where all the great benefits are waiting for us.

Remember, dopamine tells us to look for those things which were quite rare 50,000 years ago. Because these same things are now very easy to find, it makes it easy to form a habit. And these habits are often bad ones.

IT'S ALL ABOUT HABITS.

Day 8

Bad habits give short-term pleasure.

Good habits give long-term success.

Which do you want?

Here's a typical scenario. An English learner with good intentions makes the decision to finally master English. This person starts to practise a lot, watching everything on TV in English and doing lots of practice exercises. But at the end of the day, the brain thinks, "Where's the improvement? Why am I not fluent now? I've done lots of exercises in English today, and I'm not fluent!"

The brain can't observe any direct benefit in the present.

No dopamine release. The person becomes frustrated and doesn't repeat the action of practising English. No habit is formed. And they're back where they started.

The vicious circle starts again.

Mastering English isn't a sprint. It is a marathon. The sprint is easier and more accessible, but the rewards are much greater when you cross the line in a marathon.

There is another way to create a habit without the need for dopamine: repetition.

If you repeat an action enough times, it will eventually become automatic.

By repeating an action that doesn't give you any instant benefit, you can teach the brain to enjoy this new habit. Eventually, the brain starts to observe the benefits and will begin to release dopamine when you repeat that action.

That's when you can create a new habit.

Remember, bad habits are easy to form. They may feel good in the moment but they give you no benefits in the long term.

Good habits are more difficult to form. They may not feel good in the moment, but you feel good after and they give you the best, long-term results.

If you want to obtain long-term results and success, the only way is by creating the habit of working towards your goal.

Why do you think this book has thirty-one chapters to read over thirty-one days?

Because that's the time it takes to create a new habit and for that new, good habit to become more automatic.

Always remember how the primitive part of the brain works and how it tries to dominate your actions. Work with it, not against it.

Plan. Practise. Review. Reward.

And repeat.

Put most of your effort into keeping the habit of practising English, not practising English. When you have a habit of practising English regularly, you will never have to worry about success in English.

SUCCESS WILL BE INEVITABLE.

It's important to understand that it's impossible for you to be successful TODAY.

What you can do, though, is one small action that will push you a little closer to success.

Do that one action today. When you finish, give yourself a pat on the back and tell yourself you've done something good and smile. Feel good? That's dopamine.

Then do it again tomorrow. Then the next day, then the next.

Day 8

You need to create a habit, and good habits take time to form, but they are easy to keep.

Now go plant that seed and enjoy the abundance you WILL receive in the future.

PRACTICE

HOW TO REMOVE OBSTACLES

"Think in the future and act in the present."

Let's take a walk into the future. Not too far into the future, I want it to be close enough to almost feel real, and feel close enough to almost touch.

Many people think that the future is out of their hands. The reality is that the future is very much connected to the now. The future is almost completely dependent on what you do in the present.

> **YOUR PRESENT SHAPES YOUR FUTURE.**

You should think in the future, but act in the present.

I'm a big proponent of thinking long-term in order to achieve your goals. However, we know that by its very nature, the brain isn't programmed to think long-term. On the face of it, this may seem like a problem. But really, it just means that we need to practise the skill of thinking in this way.

Skills like motivation, discipline, long-term thinking and goal setting come naturally to very few people. These skills need to be practised regularly, improved and made into a habit in order to perfect them and use them to your advantage.

If a skill doesn't come naturally, a lot of people simply accept that they can't do it and never try to improve it. Instead, they focus on the skills that come naturally to them: their strengths.

Really, they should be doing the opposite.

Work on improving your weaknesses; your strengths will look after themselves.

Let me ask you a question. Have you ever thought about where you're going with your English? Why are you even learning English?

If your answer to both questions was, "I want to improve", then you need to go a lot deeper. That's not an answer that will help you long-term. It's too vague.

Another answer that will fail to help you is, "Because my boss told me I need to", or, "Because I need to in order to do…(fill the blank)".

Try to avoid the word need as it rarely helps you. Both of the above answers imply that there is something external that is imposing an obligation on you.

Try to replace the word need with the word want. A desire is far more attractive than a need.

WHY ARE YOU LEARNING ENGLISH?

Have a really long think about how to answer this question.

The interesting thing is that your answer will probably project you somewhere into the future. You should be able to visualise yourself, in five years say, having reached your goal in English.

What can you see in this visualisation of yourself in five years, with the improvement in English that you have always wanted?

Maybe you're giving a talk in your company in English in front of hundreds of people. Maybe you're speaking fluently and confidently.

Where are you in your visualisation? What are you doing? How do you feel?

Take a bit of time to develop your visualisation. The more detail, the better.

Then think of all the positive things that will come from getting to where you are in your visualisation: confidence, freedom and an enormous feeling of satisfaction.

Your practice exercise for today is to first take a pen and paper and write a brief description of your visualisation. Then I want you to write a list of positive things that will come from getting there.

Under this, I want you to write in two columns.

In Column A, write a list of everything that will help you reach that goal. These could be things like practising every day, for any amount of time, but every day; speaking out loud every day; creating and sticking with an English practice habit; incorporating English into all aspects of your life; changing the idea of study to the idea of practice and contact with the language; reading your notes for five minutes a day.

Whatever. Anything that comes to mind. Small things that will help you get there.

In Column B, write a list of things that will distract you or prevent you from getting to where you are in your visualisation. Basically, this will be a list of bad habits. Be honest with yourself here, nobody's watching!

Maybe watching a TV programme every day that you don't really enjoy, but you watch it anyway; unnecessary distractions like Facebook or WhatsApp; thinking negatively about your own skills; saying things like "I'll do it tomorrow", or "I can't", when you may not have the skill set now but you will have one day; criticising your English skills; procrastinating.

Don't look at this list as a list of sacrifices. It shouldn't be. Don't write activities down that you enjoy doing.

In fact, the items in Column B, as you can see, are not enjoyable at all.

This should be a list of unnecessary and avoidable activities, negative thoughts, and activities that conflict with the items you wrote down in the first column.

Day 8

The general rule that you need to follow in your English-learning journey is to do more things from Column A and fewer things from Column B.

That's it.

Don't worry too much about Column A just yet. The purpose of this book is to teach you what to write in Column A. But you should already have a good idea about what to write in Column B. As well as the things you first wrote in Column B, take a few minutes to look at last week. What didn't go so well? What obstacles did you come across? What prevented you from making more progress?

The answers to those questions will also go into Column B.

There are two ways to get to your destination as quickly and efficiently as possible. The first is to make the road to your destination as straight as possible. The shortest distance between two points is a straight line. The second is to remove any obstacles that are in your way.

When you have a direct path with no obstacles, there's nothing to stop you reaching your destination.

REVIEW

- *What listening are you going to do today, radio, podcast or audiobook?*
- *When is your next dictation?*
- *Which speaking practice are you doing today?*
- *Do you find it difficult to keep new habits?*
- *How many items did you write in* **column B**?

Plan

Practise

Review

Reward

> Do you want more practice? You can find an additional activity to practise the strategies from today's chapter in the free workbook. Visit www.how-to-english.com/workbook

PART II

HOW TO MAKE EVERYTHING YOU LEARN RELEVANT

*"Everything you need is right in front of your eyes.
For some reason, you just can't see it."*

DAY 9
HOW TO PRACTISE PROPERLY

*"Knowing is nothing.
Using what you know is everything."*

I'm learning to play the piano at the moment. It's a continuous process and like with most things, I will always be learning and improving. There will always be something to learn and improve.

Just like you and English.

Language and music have a lot more in common than you think. In fact, they share some of the same processes in the brain.

The parts of the brain which process individual words and vocabulary are the same parts of the brain that process melodies in music.

The parts of the brain that process grammar and the way you put words together are the same parts of the brain that process scales in music.

Words and vocabulary = melodies.

Grammar and syntax = musical scales.

Likewise, the way you learn a language has many things in common with the way you learn a musical instrument.

To learn an element of language, whether it be grammar, vocabulary or anything else, you first need to expose yourself to what you want to learn.

Then, when you know and understand what is correct, you practise it until you are able to reproduce it on your own.

What I mean by reproducing it on your own is that you can use it correctly, without any mistakes, pauses or hesitation.

When you want to learn to play a new song on a musical instrument, you do exactly the same.

You expose yourself to the correct version of the song you want to play (by listening and playing by ear or by reading the sheet music for the song), and then you practise until you are able to reproduce it on your own.

Again, without mistakes, pauses or hesitation.

Now, imagine you want to play a new song on the piano and all you do is read the sheet music. How well do you think you'll be able to play the song?

Exactly, not very well at all.

In fact, not at all.

It doesn't matter how many times you read it or listen to it. If you never touch the keys on the piano, you'll never be able to play it.

Now that seems really obvious, doesn't it?

So let's put it in the context of English learning.

Imagine you see or listen to something in English that you don't know or understand. A new word, for example.

Maybe you look up the word in the dictionary, find the meaning and write it in your notebook.

However, if you only do that, it doesn't mean that you've learned it. You have just taken the first step in the learning process: expose yourself to the correct version of what you want to learn.

If you never practise it, you'll never be able to use it without mistakes, pauses or hesitation.

Unfortunately, most English learners only take that first step in learning.

Day 9

The result is a head full of unconsolidated language that they may understand, but they can't use.

> **THE ONLY THING THAT MATTERS IS BEING ABLE TO USE WHAT YOU LEARN.**

There are two basic steps in English learning.

The first step is to acquire knowledge. You do this by exposing yourself to the correct version of what it is that you are trying to learn. You can do this by looking up a word in a dictionary if it's vocabulary, or by reading explanations of grammar elements.

The first step is to get the general understanding of what you want to learn.

Step two is to consolidate that knowledge. You do this by practising it correctly in a controlled environment. You can do this through spoken repetition, by creating example sentences, by using memory techniques to have the correct version of it extremely clear in your head.

Most English learners don't do step two. Or they only do too little of step two.

Have you ever felt frustrated because you've learned something a million times but you still can't use it?

Yes, of course you have.

Well, it's because you don't do step two or you don't do enough of step two.

Which brings us to the question, "Why don't English learners do enough of step two?"

I think they don't do enough of step two for two reasons.

First, they think that teachers put knowledge into English learners' heads. They think that if they just attend English classes, then they'll learn automatically.

Wrong.

> **ALL LEARNING COMES FROM WITHIN.**

The second reason is that step one is very easy. It's extremely easy.

It's absorbing information.

When you absorb information, you don't actually do anything.

Let me put it another way.

Which is easier, watching people run or running?

Right...

If you never do step two, you never really learn anything. If you continue to only do step one, you will never really learn anything.

Maybe that sounds a little negative.

But I mean it in a very positive way.

It means that all you need to do to really learn something is practise what you know is correct.

You know this already, but maybe you don't know the importance of it. If you don't practise what you want to learn, you will never actually learn it.

Put more importance on step two of learning and everything becomes easier.

Your aim should be to use language correctly, without any mistakes, pauses or hesitation. Step two is what will get you there.

So get off that first step and start climbing.

Day 9

PRACTICE

HOW TO PRACTISE WHAT YOU LEARN
SENTENCE CREATION & REPETITION

*"If you are not happy with your English now,
you need to change what you have been doing up to now."*

Plan, Practise, Review and Reward.

Let's focus a little on the second 'P': Practise.

When you practise, it's always to improve a particular aspect of your English. It could be to improve a skill like speaking with the daily fluency practice or listening with dictation. It could also be specific practice to improve a piece of language, like vocabulary or grammar.

As the old saying goes, *"practice makes perfect"*. Which also means that if you don't practise, your language skills can never be perfect.

Don't make the mistake of thinking that practice is studying or boring.

It's not and it shouldn't be.

Just like with the piano, practising really just means playing.

Playing with the keys on the piano is practice. Playing with words and language is practice.

It's through practice that the correct version of what you're trying to learn becomes consolidated and permanently fixed in your brain. When this happens, you can start using it in conversation.

Without practice, you will never be able to use what you know and understand. You may understand a word or grammar structure, but can you use it in a conversation?

Language is communication. And if you can't use it in a conversation, you are wasting your time.

PRACTISE UNTIL YOU CAN USE IT IN A CONVERSATION.

So how can you practise and play with language?

I'll show you an easy and effective way to do it.

I call it *sentence creation*, and it's one of the best ways to fix new words and grammar in your head.

The first and most important thing to understand is that you should practise everything you learn, no matter how small or easy you think it is.

Let's take prepositions as an example of something small, but very important.

Imagine you learn that the preposition *on* is used for days. What you need to do is create sentences that you know are correct using *on* with different days.

Here's what I would say to practise *on* by creating my own sentences.

> "I was born on April 29th. In fact, I was born on a Tuesday. I usually go running on Monday, Wednesday and Saturday. I also go to the gym on Tuesday and Thursday. If I watch a film, I prefer to watch it on a Saturday. On Christmas Day, I cook a big lunch. My wife and I go for dinner on our anniversary."

The more correct sentences you create, the more it will be fixed in your head. They should be very simple sentences. Remember, in this example we are only practising one preposition, so you don't need long and complicated sentences. You only need to use the preposition correctly.

You can do this with an idiom by saying a sentence and responding with the idiom you want to practise. You can do it with a grammar point by inventing ten or twenty simple sentences.

One of the fundamental ways the brain remembers language is by repetition. It doesn't matter what your level is, if you don't practise using basic repetition, you won't remember easily.

Day 9

You can dedicate part of your daily fluency practice to this. At the end of your fluency practice, do this exercise with a new word, phrase or grammar point that you just learned or have problems remembering or using correctly.

Alternatively, you can spend five minutes at the end of each day during *Review* to practise and review the language of the day.

If you want to write the sentences down, you can, but it's essential that you create the sentences while speaking first. Don't write down some sentences then read them out loud. Most English learners don't have problems writing, they have problems speaking and finding the correct word in their head during conversation.

Doing daily active practice for a few minutes will guarantee that you remember and you will be able to use everything that you learn.

But how can you guarantee that everything you learn will be relevant to you?

What are the best things that you, and only you, can learn?

I'll show you tomorrow.

REVIEW

- *What grammar have you learned many times but you still make mistakes with?*
- *What expressions do you understand but you can't use correctly?*
- *Which prepositions do you often make mistakes with?*
- *How can you practise them today during fluency practice?*

Plan: What, when and how you are going to practise.

Practise: Have good quality contact with English.

Review: Think about what you have learned today, what you have improved and what could be better.

Reward: Congratulate yourself and think about your achievements so far.

Do you want more practice? You can find an additional activity to practise the strategies from today's chapter in the free workbook. Visit www.how-to-english.com/workbook

DAY 10

HOW TO MAKE EVERYTHING YOU LEARN 100% RELEVANT TO YOU

"Learn what you don't know, and practise what you know."

There are two ways to go food shopping.

The first is to enter the supermarket with a trolley and fill it with everything you can see. You move down each aisle and pull items off the shelf with your whole arm into the trolley. When you finally finish, you pay (a lot) for your shopping and take it home. Then you use only the items you actually want and need, and forget about the rest.

It's not a very effective way to shop but at least *a few* of the items you bought are useful.

And you don't have to think or plan, right?

You need a lot of shopping trolleys to shop this way. You also spend much more money. It takes more time, effort and most of the items you buy go straight into the bin. After all, you don't need to buy all those items. Some of the items are useful, but most of them were completely irrelevant to you and you don't need or want them.

The result?

You spend a lot of time, money and effort, and most of what you bought is now in the bin.

The benefit is that you don't have to think or plan.

It's lazy shopping.

The second way, which is the way most people go food shopping, is to think about what you need and plan what you will buy by writing a shopping list.

Then, when you enter the supermarket, you only buy the items that are on your list. It's quick, cheap and you can guarantee that you need and want everything in your shopping trolley.

100% effective and 100% relevant to what you need

The first way is the crazy way.

The second is the right way.

It's true that you have to think a little and plan, but that thinking and planning saves a lot of time, money and effort, and it gives you perfect results every time.

That's why most people shop in this way.

Nobody shops the other way. It's totally crazy. Unfortunately, that's how most English learning happens above B1.

Remember, most of the time, the teaching material given to English learners is mostly irrelevant. You may learn some useful language, but English teaching material and course books are written for the *average English learner*.

It's not written for *you*.

As a teacher myself, I'm telling you that teachers have no idea what you should learn after B1.

No idea.

Imagine you ask me to go shopping for you, but you don't give me a shopping list. What should I buy you?

I would have no idea what to buy you.

The only way I could at least guarantee that *some* items would be relevant to you would be to buy you lots and lots of things. Of course, most of those items would go into the bin.

And this is how standard English teaching works.

So they teach you vocabulary at random or maybe teach you conditionals again.

I know…

It's not their fault. It's the only thing that they can do if they don't have a *shopping list*.

The result is that the majority of what they teach you isn't really that relevant to you as an individual English learner.

> **I THINK THAT EVERYTHING YOU LEARN SHOULD BE 100% RELEVANT TO YOU, AND ONLY YOU.**

So how can you do this? How can you make everything that you learn relevant to you, and only you?

Let's look at the two main problems of English teaching again: *what* you learn and *how* you learn.

The problem of *what* you learn is that most of the teaching material is irrelevant to you as an individual learner.

The problem of *how* you learn is that the teacher decides what you learn for you.

We can solve these two problems at the same time.

Two birds with one stone.

If you don't decide exactly what you are going to learn then the teacher will decide for you. But the only person that really knows what you need is you, not the teacher.

If you don't make your own decisions about things that affect you directly, then someone else will make those decisions for you.

The decisions that other people make regarding your learning will never be as good as the decisions YOU make about your own learning.

WHAT'S THE SOLUTION?

You need to decide what to learn, not the teacher. Nobody knows better than you.

And what should you decide to learn?

The best food shopping list only has the items that you actually want and need. It should be minimal.

There only needs to be two items on your English learning list to cover all of your needs.

Something that you want to say, but you don't know how.

Corrections of the mistakes that you make.

If you only learn these two things, you can guarantee that everything you learn will be relevant.

Why?

The first item on the list is easy to understand. If there is something that you want to say, but you don't know the correct word, it's obvious that that word is the most relevant word you can learn today. After all, you wanted to say it, but you didn't know how.

The second item on the list is also quite obvious. Improvement basically means to do something more effectively than you did before or to do it with fewer mistakes. One of the easiest ways to improve is simply to make fewer mistakes than you did before. If you can identify and eliminate mistakes that you regularly make, you will immediately improve as a result.

Easy.

Day 10

From now on, everything that you learn should fall into one of these two categories. I will show you how to look inside your own head to identify the language that you, and only you, need. I will then explain how you can learn and practise that language. That way, you will become an independent learner. You will be able to learn relevant language all the time, you will be able to control your own learning, and you will finally start making the progress that you have always wanted to make.

The solution to the problem of *what* you learn is to identify and learn only what you need and want to learn.

The solution to *how* you learn is to take control of your learning instead of depending on a teacher.

Everything you will ever need to learn already exists inside your head as empty spaces. There are gaps in your head. Little holes of knowledge. Vocabulary and grammar that you want and need but you either don't know it, or you make mistakes with it.

It is your mission to find those little holes in your knowledge, identify what you don't know, then go and learn it.

As Socrates famously said, "Wisest is he who knows he does not know."

Identifying what you don't know is the greatest learning tool you can have.

PRACTICE

HOW TO KNOW WHAT YOU DON'T KNOW
SOMETHING THAT YOU WANT TO SAY BUT YOU DON'T KNOW HOW

"It's more useful to know what you don't know than what you do know."

How's the daily fluency practice going?

By now, you should have tried all the exercises and you probably have an idea of which ones feel best and give you the best results. Which one feels best? Reading out loud, imaginary conversation, running commentary or general observation? There will probably be one which feels better and more natural than the others. It doesn't mean that the others aren't good for you. It just means that you should play with different scenarios or situations until you find a variation of each exercise that feels good.

You may think that the focus of daily fluency practice is to improve your speaking skills and become a confident English speaker. Really, the main reason I give my students this is to identify relevant language to learn. The main focus of speaking practice is to find vocabulary and grammar that you need and want to learn and practise. The secondary focus is to become an awesome English speaker.

> **IT'S A WIN-WIN SITUATION.**

Until now, you've been doing the daily fluency practice to practise speaking. That's great. Well done! From now on, the focus of the fluency practice is going to change a little.

Day 10

Remember, you don't actually learn anything from speaking. You mostly learn from listening. But speaking practice is the perfect time to find relevant language to learn, identify mistakes that you regularly make, and then work to improve these things.

And the best way to do this is by speaking on your own, as you will pay more attention to what you are saying compared to speaking with another person.

Let's look at the first item on your list of language to learn: *something that you want to say but you don't know how.*

The main focus of the daily fluency practice is to identify relevant language.

HOW CAN YOU DO THIS?

Well, you need to put a little filter between your brain and your mouth. What filter am I talking about? It's a little filter that analyses everything that you want to say before you say it.

Just as your mother used to say, *"Think before you speak"*.

As you are speaking, think about the words, the grammar and the whole sentence that you want to say. Are those words correct? Are you using the correct tense? Are the words in the correct order? Is there a better way that you could say what you want to say?

If there is a word that you want to say but you don't know how, write it down on a piece of paper or in your mobile notes, and continue speaking. Likewise, imagine you are speaking and you aren't sure if you need to use the past simple or present perfect in the sentence that you are trying to say. Think about the difference between the two tenses and if you still aren't sure, write the sentence down and continue speaking.

It will take some time to get used to in the beginning. Just as it feels strange to listen to yourself speaking out loud, it will feel strange to think about everything you want to say before you say it.

This is the skill of self-analysis, and it is one of the best learning tools you can have. After a little practice, you start to notice language that you had never paid attention to before. With an analytical mind, you start seeing learning opportunities everywhere.

Everything you need to learn is right in front of your eyes. For some reason, you can't see it. Until now...

In your daily five minutes of fluency practice, you should be able to find five things that you want to say, but you don't know how to say. Five learning opportunities.

Those five items on your list will be what you learn for the day.

HOW DO YOU FIND THE ANSWERS TO THOSE DOUBTS?

With your good friend the Internet, of course. Just write your doubt into Google and you will be able to find the answer to almost any doubt you have.

Five things to learn every day. Those five things will be the best language that you can learn. After all, you wanted to say it, but you didn't know how.

Five every day. One hundred and fifty every month. In one year, that's nearly two thousand mini-lessons that you have taught yourself. That's the best language that you can learn.

That's the first step in independent learning.

Tomorrow I will show you another way to do it...

Day 10

REVIEW

- *What does it feel like to listen to yourself speaking out loud in English?*
- *What did you learn today?*
- *What language did you find in your fluency practice that you don't know how to say?*
- *What five learning opportunities did you find today?*

Plan

Practise

Review

Reward

Do you want more practice? You can find an additional activity to practise the strategies from today's chapter in the free workbook.
Visit www.how-to-english.com/workbook

DAY 11

HOW TO FIND QUESTIONS AND DOUBTS

*"The answers to the questions in your head
are the best things you can learn."*

More than six million people live in Madrid, where I live. There are more than one and a half million houses and over nine thousand streets. That's a lot of people, houses and streets.

I know a fraction of them.

But do I need to know them all?

Thankfully, no.

If I don't need to know them all, which ones do I need to know?

Only the ones that are relevant to me. Only the people that are either part of my life or that I would like to meet and know. I only need to know the streets that help me get to where I need to go.

There are millions of things that I don't know.

But I *like* the fact that there is lots that I don't know.

It means there is lots for me to learn. I'm a very curious and inquisitive person, and I enjoy finding things that I don't know and then learning them.

And this is reflected in my teaching style.

My absolute favourite sessions with my students are my questions and doubts classes, where each person brings a question or doubt related to something they don't completely understand in English. It could be the difference in meaning between two closely related words, something they have seen or read, or anything else related to grammar, vocabulary or other aspects of English.

Everybody brings something really interesting and useful. And it is normally language that you would never find in any teaching material.

A common problem that newcomers find is that they find it difficult to think of a question or doubt.

As we take it in turns and I ask them for their questions or doubts, a newcomer will very often say, "I'm sorry, but I couldn't think of one."

My answer is always the same: "You can't just think of one, you have to find one."

The difficult part in the beginning is getting people to think on their own. Most people just aren't used to it. In most classes, the teacher thinks for you. In my classes, the learner does all the thinking.

If you sit there waiting for a question or doubt to appear, you may wait a long time. Likewise, if you try to find one in the expanse of your own brain, you'll end up looking for a long time.

And this is what makes questions and doubts sessions so fantastic. These sessions turn on the observant, analytical switch in your head, and you start seeing things that you wouldn't have seen before.

THIS SIMPLE ACTIVITY PREPARES THE BRAIN FOR LEARNING.

Newcomers often find it difficult to find a question or doubt, but the more you find, the easier it becomes to find more. The veterans in my class have the problem of having too many questions or doubts than can be resolved in one class. Their brains are on fire.

A fiery brain is good.

Day 11

A huge part – maybe the biggest part – of my methodology is getting English learners to think about English, to think about the language and its smaller parts. An effective language learner thinks about language outside of the classroom. They think about what they know, they think about what they don't know, and they think about what they need to do to learn what they don't know.

They think.

A traditional language learner will have the teacher think for them. When someone thinks for you, you will receive the least benefits.

When you think for yourself, all the rewards are for you.

Questions and doubts help you to think of relevant language to learn on a daily basis – mini lessons, so to speak.

YOU BECOME YOUR OWN TEACHER.

This is the perfect class and ideal learning environment.

A group of learners in complete control of their learning process. They bring their own material to class – questions and doubts that they have found – and ask the expert, the teacher, who simply provides answers and helps them learn.

The teacher is no longer the leader, the learners are the leaders and they are the ones who dictate their own learning. They decide what, how and how much they learn, and the vocabulary and grammar that they learn is all 100% relevant to each learner's individual needs.

Let me show you how to find questions and doubts so that you'll always have relevant language to learn.

First, I'll show you how NOT to do it.

You can't just produce a question or doubt in your head. This is the mistake that most newcomers make. The content of your brain is very large and one will not just magically appear in your head.

That's too difficult.

When a learner tells me that they couldn't find one, I generally ask, "Well, did you look for one?"

To which they often answer, "Oh... well, no."

Imagine you lose your keys. How would you go about finding them?

By looking, of course.

If you don't look for your keys, there's no way you will ever find them.

The only difference here is that you don't know what you're looking for. And that's what makes it so interesting.

> **IF YOU DON'T LOOK FOR ANYTHING, YOU DON'T FIND ANYTHING.**

But if you look for something, you always find something.

What will you find?

I can't tell you exactly, but I can tell you that it will be something worth learning.

And the answers to those questions and doubts will be the most important and relevant language that you can learn.

As I said, most people find it difficult to find questions or doubts in the beginning. This is normal. After all, you're trying to look for empty space and gaps in your knowledge. It's much easier to look for something than it is to look for empty space.

Don't worry, though, I can give you a helping hand in the beginning with the following sentences. These sentences will help you think about what you know and what you don't know, and will help you identify gaps in your knowledge and opportunities to learn.

Day 11

I don't completely understand _____ in English.

I don't know the difference between _____ and _____ in English.

I don't know how to say _____ in English.

I make mistakes with _____ in English.

Each word or phrase that you put in the gaps of each sentence is something for you to learn. Your priority should be to learn this language over all other language.

Finding questions and doubts about English makes you a more curious learner, and curiosity is one of the most powerful learning tools. Curiosity is precisely what makes children so good at learning.

Regularly fill in these sentences to find potential language to learn. Ask yourself what you need to learn and you will get the perfect answer. Nobody knows better than you.

As the old saying goes, "Ask and you shall receive."

On top of this, you have the daily fluency practice, during which you identify problems you have in real time while speaking.

The most powerful learning tool you now have is the combination of these two practices. You improve your fluency and you identify the best language for you to learn.

PRACTICE

HOW TO FIND ANSWERS TO YOUR QUESTIONS AND DOUBTS

"You never learn by speaking. You learn by asking."

Remember, in order to learn anything, there are two steps that you need to take. First, you need to understand the concept or idea of what you want to learn. Then, as we saw on Day 9, you need to practise it until you can use it without mistakes.

First, understand. Then, practise until you can use it without hesitations or mistakes.

Let's look at some examples of the self-analysis questions we saw earlier, so I can show you how to find the answers to these questions and doubts.

I don't completely understand **the present perfect** *in English.*

I don't know the difference between **in** *and* **on** *in English.*

I don't know how to say **[a word in your language]** *in English.*

Now you need to find the answers to those questions and doubts. I'm afraid I won't be with you all the time to give you the answers.

Don't worry, though. You have the next best thing: the Internet.

I don't completely understand **the present perfect** *in English.*

In the first question, we have a grammar problem. Imagine you don't completely understand the present perfect. As we saw before, you need an explanation of the present perfect in order to understand the concept. In this case, you should search for "present perfect explanation". The search results will bring up hundreds or thousands of articles, videos and maybe even audio that you can read, watch and listen to in order to get a good understanding of this tense.

I recommend getting multiple explanations of the same problem. Each explanation is an opinion. In order to really understand something, you need to receive many opinions. That way, you can then create your own understanding and opinion of what it is that you are trying to learn.

When you have your own understanding of the present perfect, you need to practise. I recommend a two-step process.

First, do some practice exercises online by searching for "present perfect exercises". The results will be many reputable websites with practice exercises. Alternatively, you can search for "present perfect exercises pdf" to get find printable versions if you prefer to have a physical copy that you can write on.

You do these practice exercises to check that you really understand the present perfect.

Secondly, you need to do fluency practice with the present perfect as the objective. This is the most important step. This is where you produce the present perfect. If you only read explanations and do practice exercises, you may understand it, but can you actually use it?

You must speak and use it to completely understand it.

*I don't know the difference between **in** and **on** in English.*

This one is simple. Simply search for "difference between **in** and **on** in English". This will bring up lots of results again. Then repeat the steps from the previous problem: explanation, practice exercises and use it by speaking.

I don't know how to say [a word in your language] in English.

In this question or doubt, you don't know how to say a particular word or phrase in English. You have the word in your own language but you are not sure how to translate it correctly.

You may think this is the easiest one, but a lot of people mistranslate or make mistakes because they don't do it correctly.

You need to look at multiple definitions, multiple contexts and multiple dictionaries to make sure you have the correct word in English. Taking so many steps helps you remember the word too. This means looking up the word in a bilingual dictionary, an English language dictionary and a bilingual context dictionary.

Your brain doesn't really understand definitions. The brain understands situation and context.

Give your brain situation and context.

And that's it. That's how you can essentially teach yourself anything.

Before we finish for the day, there's one self-analysis question that we haven't covered:

I make mistakes with _____ in English.

You make mistakes. You don't need me to tell you that. Just like everybody else, you're not perfect. But that's fine. Every mistake you make is an opportunity to learn.

But there are two types of mistakes: good mistakes and bad mistakes. Which do you make most often?

Not sure?

I'll tell you tomorrow.

Day 11

REVIEW

- *What surprised you from this chapter?*
- *What did you write in the self-analysis questions today?*
- *How do you feel different compared to 11 days ago?*
- *When did you last read out loud?*

From tomorrow onwards, you will start doing fluency practice twice per day. Write them in your practice plan now.

Plan

Practise

Review

Reward

Do you want more practice? You can find an additional activity to practise the strategies from today's chapter in the free workbook. Visit www.how-to-english.com/workbook

DAY 12
HOW TO STOP MAKING MISTAKES
GOOD MISTAKES & BAD MISTAKES

"The first time you make a mistake, it is an opportunity to learn. The second, third and fourth time you make the same mistake is when you have a problem."

When I was eleven, I really liked a girl in my class called Jane. I tried to do everything to get her attention and impress her.

Somehow, I can't remember how, I got the courage to ask her out on a date. And somehow, I can't remember how, she said yes.

"Wow!", I thought, "I did it! I've got a date with her. My first date ever!"

I then went and told everybody in my class that I was going on a date with her. That was mistake n°1.

We had arranged to meet in the local park at 5 o'clock (yes, I remember the time), and I put on my favourite black and red shell suit (not a mistake, it was 1991 and perfectly acceptable to wear shell suits).

I was a bit nervous because I wanted to impress her, but I felt confident that I had arranged the perfect date.

I thought a good date would be to show her my favourite hobby and something that I was very good at: tree climbing. That was mistake n° 2.

I took her to the best tree in the park, a willow next to the lake, and quickly climbed up the tree like a monkey. I expected her to follow, but she just leant against the tree trunk looking totally unimpressed, chewing gum.

"Hmm…maybe tree climbing wasn't the best idea after all", I thought.

My first date ever ended after five minutes.

I felt horrible, but it was nothing compared to the next day at school, when she told everybody in class about our "date".

All's well that ends well, though. We became very good friends, the other boys in the class were still impressed that I had managed to even get a date with her, and I learned never to take girls tree climbing to impress them.

YOU LIVE AND LEARN…

We all make mistakes in life. Likewise, we all want to make fewer mistakes.

However, some of the best learning experiences come from mistakes, so it's important to try to get the ideal balance between making the right mistakes and avoiding the wrong mistakes.

Let me put it more clearly. I encourage experimental mistakes and discourage avoidable, unnecessary and silly mistakes.

So let's talk about making mistakes when speaking in English. If you never make mistakes, it becomes hard to make progress.

ALL EVOLUTION COMES FROM SMALL MISTAKES.

But, there are avoidable, silly or repetitive mistakes that you shouldn't be making as an English learner. These are the ones you want to eliminate to avoid making your level sound lower than it actually is.

Which mistakes are those exactly?

Well, there are two types of mistakes: good mistakes and bad mistakes.

Good mistakes are mistakes that you make for the first time. These mis-

Day 12

takes normally correspond to a higher level. They are mistakes related to language that you don't know yet.

These are the best mistakes that you can make because each one is an opportunity to learn. The key is to be attentive and aware of when you are saying something that you aren't sure of, so that you can either ask the person you are speaking to or look it up on the Internet.

If you are doing the fluency practice correctly, you will find plenty of opportunities to learn.

Bad mistakes are mistakes that you make more than once or mistakes that correspond to a lower level. These mistakes are mistakes that you know are incorrect, but you say them anyway.

These are the worst mistakes you can make.

Here's a typical scenario in the classroom.

Student: "Spanish people is very friendly."

Me: "That's a mistake. It's *people are*, not *people is*."

Student: "Yes, I know."

Me: "Then why did you say it if you know it's incorrect?"

Student: "Because I wasn't thinking."

Me: "So what do you need to do more?"

Student: "Think?"

Me: "Exactly."

5 minutes later...

Student: "English people is very nice."

What you can see from this interaction is that although the teacher corrects the student's mistake, the student makes the same mistake again only a few minutes later. Nobody can remove your mistakes. Not a teacher, not anybody. A teacher can only tell you that you made a mistake. They can't stop you from making a mistake.

> **THE ONLY PERSON WHO CAN STOP YOU FROM MAKING MISTAKES IS YOURSELF.**

There are a couple of very important things to understand about mistakes.

The first is that the vast majority of the mistakes you make are avoidable and repetitive.

The second is that if you don't think or you don't do anything to avoid them, you will continue to make them forever.

And this is what happens in the classroom. Because most English learners depend on the teacher to correct them, they do nothing about it themselves and continue to make the same mistakes.

A teacher can correct you, but you can't always have a teacher with you to correct you. Most importantly, a teacher can never stop you making a mistake.

Prevention is always better than cure.

If you want to stop making these mistakes, YOU have to do something about it.

Day 12

PRACTICE

HOW TO IDENTIFY YOUR OWN REPETITIVE MISTAKES

"If you don't do anything to stop yourself making a mistake, you will always make the same mistakes."

Let's look at the word improvement for a moment. What is improvement exactly?

Improvement means to either produce better results than before or make fewer mistakes than before.

In the context of language learning, it could be, for example, to produce a sentence using more advanced grammatical structures or vocabulary, or to make fewer mistakes.

One of the easiest ways to improve in English is to get rid of mistakes.

HOW CAN YOU FIND THOSE MISTAKES?

That too is easy.

The good news is that most of your mistakes are repetitive ones, which means that you know most of them. In fact, I'm sure you could write a list of typical mistakes that you know you often make.

Here are four techniques you can use to identify and eliminate repetitive mistakes.

1. **Write a list**

    You already have a pretty good idea what your own repetitive mistakes are. Take a few minutes today to sit down with a pen and paper and think of all those mistakes that you regularly make.

    Do you make mistakes with vocabulary like false friends or mistranslations?

    What about structural aspects like grammar and word order?

    Are there some prepositions that you know you don't understand or use properly?

    The first ten that appear on your list will be the most obvious to you. The mistakes on this list should be your priority. Focus on eliminating them by practising the correct version. Look back at Day 9, when we covered how to practise your notes and corrections of mistakes to refresh your mind.

    You will always say what sounds most natural to you, not what is necessarily correct.

    In order to eliminate these mistakes, you need to practise the correction until it sounds more natural to you than the mistake.

2. **Speak more slowly**

    We all have a natural speed at which we like to speak. Unfortunately, most of us speak too quickly, not only in our target language, but also in our mother tongue. As a result, we often make mistakes in our target language or say things that we later regret in our own language.

    We've all done it…

    With about half of the mistakes you make when speaking in English, you know when you've made a mistake. But it's too late.

    The words left your mouth and entered the listener's ear.

    The good news is that this means they are avoidable.

    And in order to avoid those mistakes, you only need a few extra milliseconds to analyse what you're about to say before you say it.

If you speak 5% more slowly, you'll make 50% fewer mistakes.

It's like paying 5% more to receive a 50% discount.

Who wouldn't agree to that?

Speak a little bit more slowly and you'll make far fewer mistakes. But how much is 5% exactly? It just means a little bit more slowly. You will know how much slower it is because you will be able to think about the words you want to use before you say them. Normally, you think about the words you say after you say them.

Nobody will know that you are speaking more slowly. Only you. But it will give you enough time to avoid making those silly mistakes before you say them.

3. Record and listen

Do you remember when I told you that speaking on your own feels strange the first few times you do it?

It feels strange because you are listening to yourself. You normally never listen to yourself, which means that you don't really hear the words that you're using and saying.

You only hear the general message that you want to communicate to the person you're having a conversation with.

This exercise takes listening to yourself to another level.

What you do is record yourself speaking with your mobile phone. Use one of your daily fluency speaking exercises. You don't need to record all of it, just a couple of minutes.

Then, listen to it and try to find mistakes. Analyse everything you say. It's a very interesting exercise because you will hear what you say in all its detail. Those repetitive mistakes will sound very obvious and out of place. Write them down.

When you listen to English, you only normally listen for the general understanding. When you listen with the objective of finding mistakes, you suddenly start listening in a different way.

Each mistake that you hear and write down should be your priority to learn and practise.

4. Write and read

This is very similar to the previous exercise for finding repetitive mistakes that you are making. This time, you will be writing as opposed to speaking.

Generally, when we write, the words we use and sentence structures differ from when we speak. When we speak, we generally use shorter sentences and more basic vocabulary and grammar. When we write, we tend to make the sentences longer and use more variety in our language.

This means that what you write will be very different from what you say when you speak in English.

Take a pen and paper and write something in English. Try to make it as relevant as possible. For example, if you frequently write business emails in English, write an example email. If you often write to friends, write something to a friend.

What you write needs to come out naturally. The difficult aspect of this exercise is trying not to analyse what you write before you write it. Try to allow the words to flow naturally. The reason for this is that you are trying to find mistakes in what you write. The more naturally you write, the more potential mistakes you will make that you can identify and correct.

Do each of these exercises over the next few days and observe the results. Write them into your practice plan now. One per day.

Put the writing exercise (**Write and read**) in your practice plan for tomorrow, when I will show you how to do it with even more detail.

Day 12

These exercises start the process of self-analysis and self-awareness.

By becoming more self-aware and analytical, you begin to realise that everything you need to learn and make progress is actually already inside your own head.

That realisation will change everything in your learning journey.

These exercises take no more than five minutes each. If you do them regularly, you can remove 50% of all the mistakes you are making.

There are two types of repetitive mistakes: the ones you know you are making and the ones you don't know you are making.

You now have a system that you can use to identify and correct repetitive mistakes that you know you are making.

But what about those mistakes that you don't know you are making? How can you identify and eliminate those?

All will be revealed tomorrow.

REVIEW

- *What repetitive mistakes do you make?*
- *Why do you continue making the same mistakes?*
- *What are you going to do to finally stop making them?*
- *How can you practise the corrections of your repetitive mistakes?*

Do you want more practice? You can find an additional activity to practise the strategies from today's chapter in the free workbook. Visit www.how-to-english.com/workbook

DAY 13

HOW TO KNOW IF YOU ARE MAKING A MISTAKE

"Ask 'why' enough times and you find the answer to almost anything."

Once upon a time, there was a young man called Graham, who lived in a tiny little apartment in the outskirts of the city.

Graham wasn't the tidiest person.

He rarely cleaned the house or tidied up his things. He only did the washing up a couple of times a week, and only picked up his dirty clothes off the floor when he did his weekly clothes wash.

But he didn't really mind. His apartment was messy, but it was so small that it didn't really cause any drastic problems in his life.

One day, his boss gave him a promotion at work and with it, a pay rise.

Graham was over the moon. He could finally move out of his tiny home and into a bigger apartment.

In his new apartment in the city centre, Graham carried on with his messy habits. But he now found it more and more difficult to live with the mess. After all, he had more rooms and more things to organise.

He started to become more and more stressed, but he didn't realise it was the mess that was making him so stressed.

But his work continued to go well and soon after, he got another promotion.

He got another generous pay rise and moved out of his apartment into a big house in the suburbs. The new house had four bedrooms, a big garden, two bathrooms and a few other rooms.

But he carried on with his messy ways.

His house and garden were a complete disaster. Always untidy. The problem was that now his house was so big, but he was still so messy. There was no way he could ever keep it tidy, even if he wanted to.

Poor Graham.

When your house is small, it's easy to tidy. As you move into ever bigger houses without cleaning up your ways, it becomes more and more difficult to tidy, until you get to a point of no return.

When you finally get the house of your dreams, but you haven't properly looked after your house, it becomes impossible to tidy.

English learners often think that in order to move up a level, the only way is to accumulate more and more knowledge.

That's not a problem in itself, but it becomes a problem when you don't consolidate the knowledge you already have in your head.

> **INSTEAD OF TRYING TO GET A BETTER LEVEL, TRY TO BE THE BEST YOU CAN AT YOUR CURRENT LEVEL.**

That means that instead of trying to accumulate new knowledge, take some time to really consolidate the knowledge that you already have in your head.

If you're a B1 or above, you have a lot of English in your head. Much more than you realise.

But one of the reasons many English learners stop making progress at this level is because they have lots of unconsolidated knowledge in their head.

On top of this, they make the same mistakes continuously without try-

Day 13

ing to resolve them. This stops them from making progress and makes their English level appear lower than it actually is.

If you understand this book, then that's a really good indicator that you have a great level. Right now, the English "house" that you're building is already pretty big and nice. But there are certain aspects of your English that are holding you back and that stop you from realising your true potential as an English learner.

Maybe there are a few cracks in the wall that need to be filled or a water pipe has a leak in it, and it's causing problems in other parts of the house. Items in the house aren't where they should be, and there are probably certain items in your house that shouldn't even be there.

The only things preventing it from being a beautiful, tidy house are the many little problems that I mentioned above. Remove those problems and you have an exquisite house.

IT'S TIME TO CLEAN YOUR HOUSE.

The longer you leave a problem unresolved, the bigger the problem becomes and the more difficult it gets to resolve.

Typically, English learners depend on other people to correct their mistakes. This other person could be a teacher or a native English speaker that you are having a conversation with.

The problem is, you can't continue to depend on another person to correct you.

Why?

Two reasons.

Firstly, you can't have a teacher with you all the time to correct you when you are having a conversation.

Secondly, most of the time, people will only correct vocabulary mistakes and will hardly ever correct grammar ones.

WHY IS THIS?

If you make a mistake with vocabulary, people will not understand you. This is because if you say a word incorrectly, what you're saying will either mean something else or it will mean nothing.

So people will need to correct you if they want to understand you.

But with grammar it's different.

If you say, "my friend work in a bank", people will understand you.

Of course, that sentence is incorrect. It should be "my friend works in a bank", but because they understand you, they won't correct you. Why won't they correct you? Because people will feel uncomfortable correcting you in every sentence. It also kills the conversation, so they won't correct you, even if you ask them to.

That's a problem for you, because you need to speak correctly if you want to make good progress in the language. If you are able to read and understand this book, you definitely shouldn't be making these types of mistakes at this level.

So what do you do?

You get a system.

Day 13

PRACTICE

HOW TO ANALYSE AND CORRECT YOUR OWN MISTAKES

*"Instead of trying to get a better level,
try to be the best you can at your current level."*

Here is a simple system you can use to help you analyse language and correct yourself. After the analysis, you then either make a correction or choose to say something else.

Say a sentence in, for example, the present perfect right now.

Now analyse that sentence and ask yourself if it's correct. If you know the structure of the present perfect, then you should be able to say if it's correct or not without any help from anybody.

Ask yourself these questions to analyse the sentence.

What tense is it?

What structure corresponds to that tense?

What person is it? First, second or third?

Is it singular or plural?

What structure corresponds to each of those answers?

Is it affirmative, negative or interrogative?

What structure corresponds to each of those answers?

This is a quick grammatical analysis which, if you are A2 or above, you know perfectly well. You should be able to provide an answer to each of the above questions. If you can, then you know the sentence is correct. If you can't, the sentence is either incorrect or you don't completely understand how to make a sentence using that tense.

You will be slow in the beginning, but the more you practise, the quicker you'll get.

Eventually, you won't need to ask yourself all of the above questions. You can compress them all into two questions.

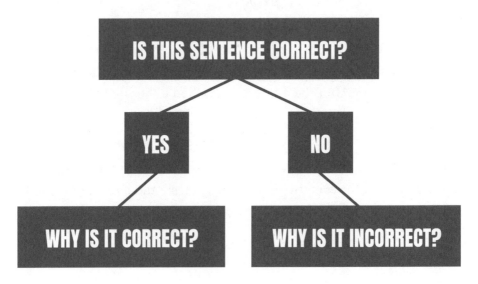

If you can provide a good answer and justification as to why it is correct, then you don't have a problem.

If you can provide a good answer and justification as to why it is incorrect, then you can make a correction or say something else.

If you think the sentence is correct but you can't answer the second question, then maybe it isn't correct or you don't completely understand it. If this is the case, you can choose to say something else or learn and practise what you are trying to say.

Start by doing this with your own writing. Your exercise for today is to write a paragraph of English. It doesn't matter what you write about, it can be about anything. Don't analyse too much as you write because

Day 13

we want to analyse the text after you write it. When you finish, ask the above questions about everything you have written. Not only tenses, but also prepositions, sentence structure and vocabulary. Circle or underline everything that you either know is incorrect or anything that you are not sure is definitely correct. Then make corrections, changes or look up what you aren't sure about on the Internet.

Slowly, you will become more accustomed to analysing and correcting on your own. Eventually, you will be able to analyse and make corrections very very quickly.

When you can do that, you can then use this technique as you speak.

You will be able to analyse everything before you even say it and make corrections before you say it.

Turn on that analytical switch in your head. It's the most powerful tool you can have to help you master English.

LEARN HOW TO CORRECT YOURSELF.

You can't depend on other people to correct you all the time.

But you can depend on yourself.

And when you depend on yourself to improve, you decide how you improve, what you improve and when you improve.

And that's when you become incredible.

REVIEW

- *What mistakes did you discover yesterday?*
- *Did you find it easy or difficult to analyse your own language?*
- *Do you find it easier to analyse your written English or spoken English?*
- *Why is that?*

Plan: What, when and how you are going to practise.

Practise: Have a good quality contact with English.

Review: Think about what you have learned today, what you have improved in and what could have been better.

Reward: Congratulate yourself and think about your achievements.

Do you want more practice? You can find an additional activity to practise the strategies from today's chapter in the free workbook. Visit www.how-to-english.com/workbook

DAY 14

HOW TO LEARN FROM EVERY TEXT YOU READ AND EVERYTHING YOU LISTEN TO

"The brain sees what it wants to see and hears what it wants to hear."

There's a really common expression we use in English to say that we know a person really well: *to know someone like the back of one's hand*. If I were talking about my friend Simon, I would say, "I know him like the back of my hand".

That got me thinking. How well do you know the back of your hand?

Yes, it's in front of you most of the time, but do you really know it in detail?

For example, without looking, can you tell me which finger is longer than the other: your ring finger or your index finger?

Probably not, right?

It turns out that the length of these two fingers differs from one person to another.

Which is longer on your hand?

You don't know, do you? They've been in front of your eyes for as long as you've been alive and you have no idea which is longer.

Why not?

"Because I've never paid attention to it", you may say.

Yes, well kind of.

What you really mean is that you've never told your brain to look and find out.

> **THE PURPOSE THAT YOU GIVE ANY ACTION IS WHAT YOU GET AS A RESULT.**

If your only purpose is to pick up an object, then that is all you do. Your brain is not interested in getting any more information that doesn't relate to the objective you give it.

If you go to pick something up, your brain won't say, "here's the object you told me to pick up, and by the way, your ring finger is longer than your index finger".

This is the same for all actions and activities in life.

When practising English, you get whatever purpose you give that activity.

Learners rarely start an activity in English with the purpose of actually learning something new. They usually start the activity with, "I want to complete this activity".

So if their only goal is to complete the activity, then that is all they do.

It sounds silly, but that's exactly what happens. They start the activity, finish it, then that's it. And they learn very little.

Let's look at listening and reading.

Every time you read or listen to something in English, how much do you learn? Do you write a list of new language and vocabulary that you would like to learn and practise?

Probably not.

> **WHY NOT?**

There is lots of language that you don't know in every paragraph of text or minute of dialogue. I always say that you can learn at least five new things from any paragraph of text or minute of dialogue in English.

Day 14

At least.

So why do you rarely find and learn new language?

Because most people start a text or listening with the objective of getting the general understanding.

If you aim to get the general understanding, then that is what you'll get.

Nothing more, nothing less.

Your brain wants to move towards the objective that you give it, and it will make it as easy as possible for you to get to that objective.

But only THAT objective. Nothing more.

You see, the brain is very good at getting the general understanding from a text or dialogue without the need to completely understand everything that is there.

> **THE BRAIN ONLY SEES WHAT IT WANTS TO SEE AND HEARS WHAT IT WANTS TO HEAR.**

It only sees what is necessary to get the general understanding and throws the rest away. It's not interested in processing extra information like tenses, prepositions or anything else that doesn't give it the general understanding.

Remember, the purpose you gave the brain was to get the general understanding. The brain will try to make the road to that goal clear.

How can it make the road clear?

By not processing unnecessary information. Anything that is not general will be thrown away.

Can you see how this powerful subconscious process works now?

All YOU need to do is tell the brain what the purpose is. When your brain has a clear purpose, it will do the rest and will help you reach that goal.

First of all, forget *general*.

General is a waste of time. *General* won't help you learn.

If you want to make real progress, actually learn useful language and really improve your English, then you have to get *specific*.

And it's so easy to do.

ALL YOU NEED IS A PURPOSE.

Next time you have contact with English, make sure that you have the purpose of actually learning something, then you will learn something.

Here's what you do. Before an activity in English, you need to say aloud, "I'm going to learn at least five new things from this". And you will see that, almost by magic, you will learn five new things.

Yes, it's that easy.

The brain will naturally move towards the objective that you give it and will make the road towards that goal clear.

If you don't look for anything, you don't find anything. If you look for something, anything, then you will always find something.

WHAT WILL YOU FIND?

I don't know.

Try it and see what you find.

What you can do is dedicate five minutes per day to looking for new language to learn and practise.

I call it purposeful practice.

It's easy.

Remember, your brain will move towards whatever purpose you give it. If you don't give the brain a purpose, it will go on autopilot and

Day 14

move towards the general understanding.

All you have to do is say, "I'm going to learn five new things from this" before you start the activity.

Now the brain has a purpose and it will actively try to find five new things, and it won't stop until it finds five new things.

Here's an example.

You have a text in front of you. Read it a first time to get the general understanding.

Now choose a paragraph and give yourself the goal of finding and learning five things, or finding five things that you don't use perfectly or fully understand.

Or how about your favourite TV series? Watch an episode. When it finishes, rewind and watch five minutes of dialogue with the purpose of learning five things. Have a notepad and pen ready or your mobile phone notes, and write down those five things as you hear them.

Now go learn and practise the list that you wrote.

From just five minutes every day of purposeful practice, you can learn five new things every single day.

What's great is that those five items will be 100% relevant. After all, you chose to learn them.

You decide what you learn, because only you know what you need to learn.

PRACTICE

HOW TO LOOK FOR AND FIND NEW LANGUAGE

"If you don't look, you don't find."

There's the old fable that talks of two friends, Bill and Ben, out camping in the wilderness. They have dinner by the campfire, then head to the tent to sleep for the night.

After a while, Bill wakes his friend up and says, "Ben, look up and tell me what you see".

Ben answers, "Millions of stars."

"And what does that tell you?", asks Bill.

"Well, it tells me that the universe is huge beyond comprehension, and we are small and insignificant. It also tells me that, as it's a clear sky, the weather will probably be good tomorrow. Why? What does it tell you?"

Bill pauses for a moment before replying, "It tells me that someone has stolen our tent."

A funny story, and so true. It happens to all of us. It's so easy to completely miss what is in front of our very eyes. It is only when we look with a purpose that we actually see what is there.

As well as what isn't there...

So let's do a little purposeful practice together.

I want you to go back to the first page of this chapter, Day 14, and read it again. Each time you read it, I will give you a purpose and objective. With each purpose, you will find and potentially learn something new.

Day 14

Without a purpose, you only get the general understanding and you learn very little. When you give the brain something to look for, you always find something.

Let's begin.

The first purpose you will have is to read the first page of this chapter and underline five things that are new to you. They can be expressions, phrasal verbs, a grammatical structure, general vocabulary…anything. Be careful because the exercise isn't to find five things that you don't understand. I know you understood the chapter. Ask yourself, "Would I write this sentence in the same way?" If the answer is no, there's something in the sentence that you can learn.

So go back now, read the first page again and underline or write down five new things for you to learn and practise. I'll see you back here in a minute.

Done?

Great! I hope you found some useful language.

Now I want you to read the first page of this chapter again, but this time I want you to find and circle every preposition.

With every preposition that you find, I want you to think about what the function of each preposition is. Is it part of a phrasal verb and if it is, do you know this phrasal verb? Is it a dependent preposition? Is it connecting two nouns? Is it part of a phrase? Does a gerund follow it? Just take a moment to look and analyse each preposition and its function in the sentence.

Go.

How did you get on?

Right then, here's the last one. This time, I want you to read the first page of this chapter again and identify each tense.

You will know each tense without any difficulty, but the idea is for you to think about each sentence and ask yourself if you would use the same tense in the same sentence. Is this sentence written in a different tense in your language? Do you have problems with this tense? Which tense is most frequently used?

Off you go.

Done?

And there you have it. That's purposeful practice. You can see that simply by giving an activity a purpose, you can discover many things. Without a purpose or objective, you simply complete the task as quickly as possible and miss many learning opportunities.

It's similar to the city you are currently living in. How many times do you look up at the buildings that surround you and really see what's around you?

Probably not that often. Your brain thinks it has seen everything that is relevant in your city, so you stop looking around.

But when you visit a new city, that's exactly what you do. You look around, you take it all in and you try to learn.

There are still many things to discover in the place you live, no matter how long you have lived there.

Next time you go outside, take a look around and try to find something new or simply observe the world around you. I can guarantee you'll see something that you haven't seen before.

When you do this with language, you always find and learn something new. You discover that there is an opportunity to learn with every contact you have with English.

And there always has been an opportunity to learn something new. It was in front of your eyes the whole time. You just weren't looking.

As the old saying goes, "I was blind but now I can see."

Day 14

REVIEW

- *What are you going to do with the language that you found in the purposeful practice exercise?*
- *Did the text look different each time you read it?*
- *How can you use purposeful practice every day?*
- *Which fluency exercise are you going to do today?*
- *When is your next dictation?*

Plan

Practise

Review

Reward

> Do you want more practice? You can find an additional activity to practise the strategies from today's chapter in the free workbook. Visit www.how-to-english.com/workbook

DAY 15

HOW TO IDENTIFY YOUR WEAKNESSES
WHAT'S YOUR BIGGEST WEAKNESS?

*"Focus on improving your weaknesses.
Your strengths will look after themselves."*

So you have decided that you are going to tidy your house.

That's great news!

Where are you going to start exactly?

The first and most logical thing to do is establish which room is in the worst state. Which room is holding the rest of the house back? That's the best place to start. After all, why tidy and clean a room that's already clean and tidy?

With a house, it's easy to establish which room is the one that needs the most work immediately. You can see which one is messiest and simply start there.

With English skills, it can be a little harder to work out. Your main weakness isn't as physical or visual as a house that needs tidying.

To find out, you can start by asking yourself a few questions.

What would you say is your biggest weakness in English? Which skill is your biggest obstacle in making progress? If you could make one aspect of your English perfect, which one would you choose?

Generally, you will find that you have the same answer for each of the above questions.

And you would think that it's easy to find the answer. The truth is that although you find an answer to the above questions very quickly, it may not be the correct answer.

> **IDENTIFYING YOUR WEAKNESSES ISN'T ALWAYS AS SIMPLE AS IT FIRST SEEMS.**

I once asked a student of mine, Sara, what she thought her main weakness was. Here's how the conversation went.

"So, Sara, what do you think your biggest weakness is?"

She answered immediately, "Speaking in English."

"Why do you have problems speaking in English?"

"Well", she continued, "I find it difficult to get the words out of my mouth, particularly in meetings. I worry that people will ask me questions and I won't be able to answer them, so I don't speak. I also worry that people will hear my mistakes and think my English level is low."

Are you thinking what I was thinking?

Right. Her weakness isn't actually speaking. It's something else.

In fact, it's the same weakness that many language learners have. And the same weakness that a majority of the population has: a fear of what others think of us.

When many people say that their weakness is speaking, what they're really saying is that.

Fear of what others will think of them.

That fear stops them from speaking.

Various studies have shown that public speaking is consistently first or second in rankings of biggest fears. It's a natural fear, and it reflects the fact that we humans are group animals, and the group's opinion of us is very important to us.

Day 15

Now when I say *scared of speaking English*, I don't necessarily mean that you are trembling and unable to speak. I think 90% of English learners have this fear, but on different levels. Some do tremble and physically cannot speak, but most don't. Most simply don't feel comfortable or say "I don't really like speaking in front of others in English" or "I prefer to let others speak" or "If I'm not sure of what I'm saying, I prefer to just stay quiet". But they wouldn't say they are scared.

But if a thought is stopping you from speaking as much as you would like to, then that's fear, and you should work on improving it.

So the advice I gave Sara was not to speak more. She knows she needs to speak more, but fear is stopping her.

The best thing that Sara can do is overcome her fear. When she can do that, then she can really improve her speaking skills. Until she does that, her fear of speaking will always stop her from improving.

The conversation with another student of mine, Eva, went something like this.

"So, Eva, what's your biggest weakness as an English learner?"

"Grammar. Definitely grammar", she quickly replied.

"And what problems do you have with grammar?"

"When I speak, I make a lot of mistakes with grammar."

She identified the mistakes she was making perfectly. She almost always used only the present simple when speaking, even when she was speaking in the past or future. I then asked her multiple grammar questions and what surprised her was that she got them all correct.

Not one grammar mistake.

Exactly. Her main weakness is not grammar, but something else.

Eva was very outgoing and sociable. She loved talking. So much so that when she spoke, she only thought about getting her idea across. She never thought about the correct structures to use when speaking.

IF YOU DON'T THINK, YOU MAKE MISTAKES.

My advice to her wasn't to study grammar. That's the last thing she should do. She knew grammar perfectly. If she had studied grammar, it wouldn't have helped her at all and she would have wasted her time. All she needed to do was be more aware of what she was saying and think a little about the correct structures to use when speaking.

Problem solved.

Sara's weakness wasn't speaking but rather a fear of speaking. They are two very different problems.

Eva's problem wasn't with grammar but rather the fact that she didn't think when she was speaking and made grammar mistakes. They are not the same weakness at all.

What this means is that you really need to go quite deep when you ask yourself the question of what your weakness is. Don't accept your first answer as the absolute truth. It probably won't be. You need to ask yourself why that is your weakness and find the deeper reason. The deeper you can go, the more exact your answer will be, which will help you identify how you should practise.

When you practise, your focus should be to practise that which you have difficulties with.

Slowly, those obstacles will no longer be in your way and you travel down the road to fluency with little difficulty.

Day 15

PRACTICE

HOW TO USE DRILLS TO MAKE MASSIVE PROGRESS

"Humans, like electricity, prefer to follow the path of least resistance. But with less resistance comes less reward."

Usain Bolt once famously said that the 100m sprint is easy.

The hard part is the hours of intense training that his coach puts him through every day. It's everything the spectators don't see that's difficult, not the sprint itself.

Of course, it's what happens out of the Olympic stadium that determines his progress.

And the same goes for language learning. It's not what you do in the classroom that determines how much you progress. It's what you do when you're not in the classroom.

This, of course, means that it's not the teacher or the classes that decide how much you learn and how much progress you make.

It's you.

Your progress depends on the amount of practice and quality of the practice that you do on a daily basis.

WHAT IS PRACTISE EXACTLY?

Practice basically means to repeat a particular action with the idea of improving.

For example, you can't practise tennis because it's a sport. But you can practise an element of tennis, for instance, your serve.

Practice is conscious repetition with the aim of improving.

The easiest way to improve through repetition is by doing drills.

A drill is just that: a repetitive practice exercise focusing on one particular skill or, in the case of English, a particular language point.

Usain Bolt does running drills, with each drill focusing on improving one aspect of his running to make him an overall better runner.

An effective English learner does drills, with each drill focusing on improving one aspect of their language skills to make them an overall better English speaker.

Drills are great because they allow you to actively practise the language. Actively practising the language is the only way that you can remember and - more importantly - use the language.

The daily practice exercises from now on will be in the form of drills. I will give you short and intense drills for each of the skills in English. You can do them anywhere in a few minutes and they will completely change the amount of progress that you make.

Today's drill is something I call *tense transformation*.

Here's how you do it.

Say a short sentence in the present simple. For example, *I eat bananas*.

Now repeat the sentence in all the present, past and future tenses.

This is what it should look like.

> "*I eat bananas. I'm eating bananas. I've eaten bananas. I've been eating bananas. I ate bananas. I was eating bananas. I'd eaten bananas. I'd been eating bananas. I'll eat bananas. I'm going to eat bananas...*"

Then change to the second person and repeat.

When you finish that, do it again in third person singular.

It takes no more than a couple of minutes. In the beginning, you will be slow and you should check that what you're saying is correct using the techniques we covered on Day 13.

And as always, you must say the sentences out loud, not in your head.

As you practise, you will notice that the tenses start to flow effortlessly.

When that happens, you won't need to think as much while you speak. You will make fewer mistakes and you will feel more fluent.

And progress in English is exactly that: fewer mistakes and more fluency.

REVIEW

- *What is your biggest weakness in English?*
- *Are you sure it is that and not something a little deeper?*
- *How can you start to improve it?*
- *When are you going to start doing the short drills?*
- *Which tenses or conjugations do you think you will have problems with?*
- *What improvements have you noticed from doing the daily fluency practice?*
- *What listening without visuals did you do today?*

Plan

Practise

Review

Reward

> Do you want more practice? You can find an additional activity to practise the strategies from today's chapter in the free workbook. Visit www.how-to-english.com/workbook

DAY 16

MOTIVATION, SELF-DISCIPLINE AND HABITS (PART 2)
HOW TO ALWAYS BE MOTIVATED

"If there is no goal, where do you kick the ball?"

When I bought my piano, my intention was never to become an expert pianist.

I am definitely not an expert pianist!

All I wanted to do was learn to play my favourite songs and musical pieces.

What about you? Would you like to play an instrument?

Maybe not…

But would you like to be able to play your favourite songs on an instrument?

I'm sure most of you would.

Simply having a reason why you are learning something completely changes how attractive the learning process appears.

Learning something big like a language or musical instrument follows a completely different process compared to say, learning to ride a bike or learning to drive a car, which have a clear end point.

Learning a language or musical instrument don't really have an end point. There is no moment at which you can say, "There! I've done it. I've learned English!"

When you are learning big topics or subjects that have no end point, it's important that your attitude to learning reflects the process.

What I mean by this is that you should not focus on the end goal of learning English.

Because there is no end goal.

Which means you will never reach it.

Which means you'll get frustrated.

Which means you may give up.

DO NOT GIVE UP.

Instead, change your focus.

Focusing on learning English (which means the whole language!) can be very intimidating.

Change your focus to having a purpose (a reason why) and milestones (small steps in the learning process).

Without a purpose, the whole thing seems useless and pointless.

Let's go back to the piano for a moment.

I never think about learning to play the piano extremely well.

My only interest, for now at least, is to learn my favourite songs and pieces.

My purpose is to learn to play and sing along to my favourite songs. And if I learn enough songs, I will eventually be a very good pianist as a natural result of knowing many songs.

And my milestones are the individual songs that I learn to play.

These milestones are great short-term goals that I can work towards and achieve pretty effortlessly in a week or two.

Day 16

So I'm always making progress, and I never get worried about the end goal, because there isn't one.

All I need to do is sit down for a bit today and practise a particular part of the song I'm working on.

Nothing more. As the old saying goes, "Slowly slowly, catchy monkey."

> **ONLY THINK ABOUT THAT ONE ACTION THAT YOU CAN DO TODAY.**

If you do it, then do it again tomorrow, eventually you'll get closer to your goal and stay motivated.

If you worry about reaching (or not reaching) an end goal, the brain will find excuses not to get there.

The brain doesn't like focusing on big end goals.

I'm not saying you shouldn't have big end goals. I think you should; they are essential.

But you shouldn't only have big end goals.

Start with a big end goal but you should also know that you may never reach that goal. But that's ok. More important than that is reaching milestones and making progress.

Imagine a football match. When the referee blows the whistle to signal the start, the player doesn't try to kick the ball straight into the goal. That's far too intimidating and almost impossible.

No. Instead, the player passes the ball to another player and works to slowly move closer and closer to the goal.

Each successful pass is a milestone.

Milestones are actions. And milestones are progress.

ONLY ACTIONS AND PROGRESS MATTER.

And if you aren't making progress in English, that means you are losing English.

So how can you stay motivated to keep making progress towards your goals?

Well, that's related to the magic of motivation itself.

It is not reaching the end goal that keeps you motivated. That's the strange thing about motivation. In fact, when you reach your goal, whatever it is, that's when you have the highest chance of giving up. You feel great satisfaction from reaching your goal, but you don't feel motivated.

Why?

Because you've reached your goal.

What do you have to move towards now?

Nothing. You've reached your goal so you don't have anything to move towards.

This is exactly what happens to many people on a diet when they reach their target weight. As soon as they reach it, they lose motivation and put weight back on.

Why is this?

The word motivation itself is actually related to *moving* towards your goal, not reaching it.

That means that it is not reaching the goal that makes you motivated, but rather the feeling that you are moving closer to your goal. You feel most motivated when you feel that you are moving closer to your goal, making progress and hitting milestones.

Day 16

Progress is motivation. Reaching small milestones as regularly as possible is motivation.

The solution?

Make progress every day, hit a milestone every day, and you will always feel motivated.

PRACTICE

HOW TO MASTER SENTENCE STRUCTURE
AFFIRMATIVE, NEGATIVE & INTERROGATIVE

"Practise what you find most difficult."

Boiled eggs, bananas and nuts.

This is the packed lunch I have every working day.

I usually include a handful of raisins and maybe even a couple of apples if I'm feeling crazy. But always boiled eggs, bananas and nuts.

I generally don't have time to go home to cook anything or go to a restaurant to have lunch, so I have this.

I love it.

It's small but filling, nutritious, and I don't need a knife or fork to eat it, so I can carry it around and eat it anywhere I want.

The fact that it is small and compact make it an incredible meal. To fill your belly, it's not essential that you eat a large meal.

Likewise, to practise English effectively, some of the best practice you can get is by doing five-minute drills on the way to work or while doing the dishes. Just take a few minutes of your unfocused practice time and dedicate it to something that gives great results and fills your brain.

Just like the way my packed lunch fills my belly.

Day 16

Today's drill is called *Affirmative, Negative and Interrogative*.

Similar to yesterday's *Tense Transformation* drill, you make changes to a simple sentence. As the name suggests, you make the affirmative, negative and interrogative of a sentence, make a small change in the sentence and then repeat.

Here's an example.

I write every day. I don't write every day. Do I write every day?

Then change to third person singular.

He writes every day. He doesn't write every day. Does he write every day?

Then change the tense.

She has written every day. She hasn't written every day. Has she written every day?

Past simple.

I wrote every day. I didn't write every day. Did I write every day?

Present perfect continuous.

I have been writing every day. I haven't been writing every day. Have I been writing every day?

And so on.

When you don't have good fluency, you have problems finding the correct words and structures in your head. You pause, hesitate and think too much while you speak. And of course, if you don't practise finding the correct words and structures, you will continue to have problems with it.

THIS PRACTICE ELIMINATES THAT PROBLEM.

It makes it easy for you to find the correct words and structures.

As you get better and faster, you can change to progressively more complex sentences, like conditionals.

You can also do this drill with any written English. With each sentence in the text you are using, change the structure from affirmative to negative, and negative to interrogative.

It's a simple drill and feels more like play than work. But the results are great and it makes you fast on your feet when you're speaking. You will rarely have doubts about the structure of sentences if you practise this regularly.

Many English learners make unnecessary mistakes when they form sentences in the negative or interrogative. Practising those structures in a controlled way helps you master them and gets rid of these mistakes.

In the beginning, you will need to do it slowly to make sure you are not making a mistake with the structures. However, you will start to make progress very quickly.

Every time you do it, you'll notice the progress, particularly if you use more and more complex sentences.

And progress is motivation.

Day 16

REVIEW

- *How have you made progress in your English today?*
- *Think back to before you started reading this book. How do you feel now compared to then?*
- *What do you now know that you didn't before?*
- *How has your fluency improved since Day 1?*
- *When are you going to do the Affirmative, Negative and Interrogative drill?*

Plan

Practise

Review

Reward

> Do you want more practice? You can find an additional activity to practise the strategies from today's chapter in the free workbook. Visit www.how-to-english.com/workbook

PART III

HOW TO MASTER VOCABULARY, GRAMMAR AND PRONUNCIATION

"The brain is very good at understanding language on its own, given the right environment."

DAY 17

HOW TO READ BOOKS IN ENGLISH
THE KING OF ALL VOCABULARY EXERCISES

"The best kind of learning is when you don't know that you're learning."

I was lying on a sun lounger next to the swimming pool in the baking heat, with only the sound of the crickets in the August air.

I started eating the figs that I had just pulled from the branches of the fig tree next to the pool.

"I have earned them!", I thought.

I had just finished reading my first novel in Spanish and felt extremely proud of myself. I also felt great because I had learned a lot of new language.

It was only while reading that I realised what I really needed to learn in Spanish to truly make progress.

When you read, you actually see the language, and really notice the small details that you wouldn't normally notice.

In that first book, I saw and learned so much vocabulary it was incredible. It changed everything in my learning process. I saw and learned verb tenses that I had never seen before. People had probably used these tenses when speaking to me but I simply didn't hear them. After all, the brain sees what it wants to see and hears what it wants to hear.

And this is sometimes the problem when you only rely on speaking to improve.

Speaking is great and essential for fluency, and most English learners definitely need more of it. But you don't often actually learn much new language when in a conversation.

You're too busy listening or speaking. You don't have time to really absorb new language, process it, think about it and learn it.

In a conversation, there's so much language that simply goes in one ear, and straight out of the other.

Why?

In a conversation, your brain only listens to the minimum it needs to understand the overall context of what the speaker is saying.

As a result, we miss lots of language in a conversation.

Reading in your target language is great for practising verb tenses and grammar in general, but the greatest benefits of reading are for learning vocabulary.

IT IS THE KING OF ALL VOCABULARY EXERCISES.

Let me show you why and how the process works in the brain.

When you read a novel, your brain processes around 80,000 words, as well as the structures that connect all those words.

That's a lot of words.

Don't worry, you don't need to learn all those words. You will already know most of them and the majority will be repeated.

In a novel, a good writer will try to paint a picture for you so you feel like you are inside the book.

To do this, they use a lot of adjectives, adverbs, idioms and expressions, as this vocabulary is what we use to describe situations in more detail.

The writer does this to create an image in the reader's mind. The brain loves working with images to remember and understand the world. This is why most of your thoughts, dreams and memories are images.

The words that the writer uses to create those images really expand your vocabulary, and the structures that the writer uses to connect all those words really help solidify your understanding of grammar and sentence structure.

It really is some of the best practice you can do. The amazing thing about it is that it doesn't feel like you are practising English. And that is extremely important. At B1 and above, you really shouldn't be spending any time at all actually studying. Studying was when you were at school or your first few levels of English study. Change the way you think about practising English from study to play.

Reading is enjoyable and relaxing. It is not studying. In fact, when you read in English, the main focus isn't even to improve your English. The main focus is to enjoy yourself and relax.

Improving your English is secondary.

Although improving English is secondary, it is one of the few practice exercises that will take your English to another level.

As a teacher, I always know when one of my students reads in English regularly. They have a range of vocabulary and control over their use of English that the other students simply do not have.

READING CHANGES EVERYTHING.

So you now know that reading in English should be a regular part of your life. But how do you choose the right book to read in English?

The best way to find the right book is by filtering out the wrong books.

There is nothing more frustrating than buying a book in another language only to discover that it is either too difficult to read or too boring.

Remember, your priority when choosing a book is not English, but rather to enjoy a good book.

To filter out the bad books, you need three filters.

First, go to a bookshop or online and go to the section where you can find books in English.

When you see a book, first ask yourself the question, "Would I read this book in my language?"

If the answer is "no", put the book down and find another.

If the answer is "yes", go to the next filter.

Now, read the blurb (the short overview of the story on the back of the book) and ask yourself if it still looks interesting.

No? Put the book down.

Yes? On to the last filter.

This is the most important filter. You need to read the first three or four pages to see how much you understand. I generally say that you need to understand around 80% in order to be able to read the book comfortably and without interruption.

How much is 80%?

IT'S A FEELING.

After reading those first few pages, put the book down and ask yourself if you could explain to another person more or less what has happened in those three or four pages. You will know if you've understood enough.

It's very important to do this as each writer has a particular style. Some

Day 17

are easy to read. Others use very complex structures and words, or describe everything in such detail that it makes the book difficult to follow if it's not in your own language.

If the book passes the three filters, buy the book.

When you read a book in English, the priority is not to practise English. The primary focus is to relax and enjoy yourself. That means that if there is a word or expression that you haven't seen before or don't understand, don't put the book down to look up the word in the dictionary. Just carry on reading. You won't understand every word, but that's OK. As long as you understand 80%, you will still be able to get the general idea. A good idea is to underline or circle the word or expression, which you can then look up when you finish reading. Don't break the flow of reading, or you won't enjoy your book, which is the only real purpose of reading.

If there are too many words that you don't understand, it means you probably aren't reaching the 80% comprehension and it may not be the right book for you.

Each time you see a new word in a book, your brain will try to decipher its meaning and this will help you both understand it and solidify it in your memory.

If you just look for a word in a dictionary, you may get the meaning of that word, but you probably won't remember it or use it because you don't know how to. You haven't seen it in context.

Only the sentence in the example they give you in the dictionary, and that's not enough.

> **THE BRAIN IS VERY GOOD AT UNDERSTANDING LANGUAGE ON ITS OWN, GIVEN THE RIGHT ENVIRONMENT.**

Reading is the perfect environment to fill your brain with new language and vocabulary without the need to actually study it.

You will learn things without even realising it.

So go out and buy that one book you have been wanting to read, and read it.

After you finish this book, of course.

Day 17

PRACTICE
HOW TO EXPAND YOUR VOCABULARY
BIG BANG VOCABULARY BUILDER

"Everything you need to learn and make progress is actually already inside your own head."

This is one of my favourite exercises to help increase your range of vocabulary.

I call it the *Big Bang Vocabulary Builder* because you create new words from one central root word. This central root word expands to create new words, just as a focal point expanded to create new matter at the time of the Big Bang.

What you do is take a word and say what word class it is: verb, noun, adjective or adverb.

When you determine what it is, you then find the other forms of that word that correspond to the other classes. Sometimes, the root word may have multiple nouns or adjectives. Sometimes, the root word may not have an adverb.

Here's an example. Take the word *employ*.

What word class it is?

Verb. Exactly.

Now find the nouns and adjectives that correspond to the word *employ*.

The nouns are *employment, employability, employee* and *employer*.

The adjectives are *employed* and *employable*.

You can even play with negative prefixes and opposites like *unemployed*.

Here's another one: *strong*.

Word class?

Right. Adjective.

Noun: *strength*. Verb: *strengthen*. Adverb: *strongly*. This word doesn't take a negative prefix so we can use its opposite and do the same: *weak*. Noun: *weakness*. Verb: *weaken*. Adverb: *weakly*.

Find new words and repeat. For some words, you will already know the answer and for others, you may need to use a dictionary.

For every new word that you learn, you will learn all the other words related to it. That's what makes it such a good exercise. You learn new words, but it also helps you remember those new words by using them. It also helps you organise those words in your head.

Do it with every new word you learn as well as with the words that you already know and you will multiply the number of words you know. This is the ideal practice to do when you are on public transport or walking. It's quick, easy and it will have a huge impact on your range of vocabulary.

It's called the *Big Bang Vocabulary Builder* for good reason.

Day 17

REVIEW

- *What changes in your English have you noticed from regularly reading this book?*
- *Do you find it easier to read compared to the first few days?*
- *How many times have you looked for words or expressions in a dictionary?*
- *Do you find it hard to organise vocabulary in your head?*

Plan

Practise

Review

Reward

> Do you want more practice? You can find an additional activity to practise the strategies from today's chapter in the free workbook.
> Visit www.how-to-english.com/workbook

DAY 18

HOW TO INCREASE YOUR WORKING VOCABULARY

"Self-analysis is the key to self-improvement."

My fish and seafood vocabulary in English is quite limited. I only know and use the names of the few most common types of fish and seafood that we typically eat in England.

In fact, I know more words in Spanish related to fish and seafood than in English.

"Why is that?", you may ask.

Well, I never really ate much fish or seafood when I was living in England. I eat much more in Spain, where there is more culture of eating seafood.

But my seafood vocabulary isn't completely limited in English.

If I hear words related to fish or seafood in English, I will understand them, but they are not words that I have in my own working vocabulary.

What is a person's working vocabulary?

A person's working vocabulary is the set of words and phrases that the person uses regularly. The person will understand many more words but they won't use them when they communicate.

Which words make up a person's working vocabulary?

Words that are relevant to that person. Words that are relevant to you are generally the words that you regularly use because you are interested in them or they are important to you for some reason.

RELEVANT VOCABULARY

Each person has their own set of words, phrases, idioms and expressions that reflect how they like to express themselves.

Your priority when learning vocabulary is to learn these words and expressions and not worry too much about all other vocabulary.

The words in your working vocabulary are the words that you will use more than any others.

Learning what I call *general vocabulary* is also important, but not as important as learning the specific words that form your working vocabulary.

General vocabulary is for comprehension and understanding.

Specific words that form your working vocabulary are the words that you will use when you communicate.

That's why I don't need to learn all the words for the different types of seafood that exist because I don't talk about them. It's a waste of time to learn and practise those words. As long as I understand them, that's all that matters.

I love running. I know quite a lot about running and have lots of vocabulary to talk about different aspects of the sport. I know very little about sports that don't interest me.

General vocabulary is about comprehension.

Working vocabulary is about usage.

To put it another way, general vocabulary is about the words that you receive through listening and reading in English. What I call *English input*.

Day 18

Working vocabulary is about the words that you use when you speak and write in English. What I call *English output*.

Nobody teaches this difference, but it's one of the most important things you can learn. If you don't learn the difference between learning general language and specific language, you end up learning nothing.

Nobody can teach you your personal working vocabulary. There's not one teacher in the world that can know exactly what vocabulary you want and need to learn. So what vocabulary do teachers teach you? General vocabulary. Some of that vocabulary will be relevant to you, but most of it will not.

I call it *the shotgun effect*. A shotgun doesn't have a bullet like a normal gun. It has a cartridge which contains hundreds of little bullets - or pellets, as they are called. This means that to shoot your target, you don't need to aim very well because you can guarantee that at least a few of the hundreds of pellets will hit your target.

That also means that the vast majority of the pellets will not hit the target.

It's exactly the same effect when a teacher teaches you general vocabulary. Most of that vocabulary will not be relevant to you, but at least the teacher can guarantee that some of the vocabulary will be relevant.

I think that's a waste of time.

An example of this is when you have an English class about idioms and expressions. What normally happens is that the teacher will teach you a list of idioms or expressions and their meaning. Then what happens is that the student leaves the class and never uses them again.

Why?

There are thousands of idioms and expressions in English. Do you need to learn them all? No, only the ones that you use in your own language, as they are the ones that reflect the way you like to express yourself.

The best way to learn idioms and expressions is to write down the idioms and expressions that you most use in your own language. Then go find their translations.

No teacher knows what specific vocabulary you need for your own working vocabulary.

Only you.

You need to find relevant vocabulary and learn it.

In Part 3, the focus is how to learn both general language and specific language. Both are important, but the way you learn one is totally different from the way you learn the other.

Day 17, for example, was about learning general vocabulary by reading, which is the absolute best way to do it.

Today, we will look at how to learn the specific vocabulary that makes up your working vocabulary.

Your focus should always be to learn vocabulary, grammar and pronunciation that form part of your English output. After all, they are what you will use when you communicate.

> **LEARNING SPECIFIC VOCABULARY IS NOT THE SAME AS LEARNING GENERAL VOCABULARY.**

The key to learning general vocabulary is to practise it passively. That means that when you are practising it, your main goal isn't to learn vocabulary. Learning vocabulary is secondary.

Take reading fiction, for example. Your goal when you read a good book is not to learn vocabulary. Your goal is to relax and enjoy yourself. However, you also learn a lot of vocabulary passively because you read thousands and thousands of words.

Learning specific vocabulary is different.

To learn specific vocabulary, you need to practise it actively. That means that your goal is to find relevant vocabulary and practise it using the drills I give you each day.

You will learn general vocabulary automatically by reading and listening to English regularly.

To learn specific vocabulary, you have to look for it, learn it and then practise it.

The first thing you need to do is identify the vocabulary that you want to learn.

The purpose of the daily fluency practice is to improve your speaking skills and to identify relevant vocabulary to learn. This is very important. It means that every time you do fluency practise, you should have two goals: to improve your fluency and to find relevant vocabulary to learn.

WHICH VOCABULARY SHOULD YOU LEARN?

1. Words and expressions that you don't know how to translate from your language into English.
2. When you don't know the difference between two related words, you should learn and practise both words.
3. Anything that you want to say, but you don't know how.
4. Vocabulary that you know you make mistakes with. Learn and practise the corrections to those mistakes.
5. Vocabulary that you find in a text or listening. If you are not sure how to do this, go back and read Day 14 again.

When you identify a word or expression, the next and most important thing to do is practise it. Practise that vocabulary using the daily drills that I show you.

With every new relevant word that you learn, you remove an obstacle in communication.

Without any obstacles, you have real fluency, and all of the problems that you have speaking in English simply disappear.

Day 18

PRACTICE

HOW TO FIND RELEVANT VOCABULARY

"You don't learn vocabulary by looking at words in a dictionary. You learn vocabulary by practising it."

Let's look at the process of learning vocabulary.

When you look up a word in the dictionary and see what it means, you may understand it, but will you be able to use it in the future?

The only thing that matters is being able to use it in the future.

Let's take a typical day as an example of how this works in the brain.

In a typical day, your brain is exposed to continuous stimulation. You see, hear, smell and feel thousands of things throughout the day.

How many of those things do you remember at the end of the day?

Very few.

Only the things that stand out get remembered.

Which things stand out?

Those which your brain considers important.

With English learning, you can make language stand out by simply using it. I call it *playing with words*, and really it just means manipulating the words, creating sentences with them and connecting them to other related words

When you see the meaning of the word and a translation into your language, that's not the moment that the learning process ends, it's when the learning process really begins.

If you just look up a word in the dictionary and write it down in your notebook, you will forget it.

Guaranteed.

By practising and playing with the vocabulary, you can transfer the vocabulary over to your long-term memory, which will allow you to use it in the future.

People will say things like, "I need to practise vocabulary, but I don't know how", yet they are completely surrounded by vocabulary at all times.

Take a moment now to look around.

What can you see?

Can you say all of those things in English? Are there verbs, phrasal verbs, adjectives or expressions associated with the objects you can see?

I'm looking at the trousers I'm wearing right now. Here's some vocabulary related to the noun *trousers*.

Nouns: trousers, leg, pocket, zip, waist, belt…

Adjectives: baggy, tight, fitted…

Verbs: wear, fit, suit, iron…

Phrasal verbs: zip them up, turn them inside-out, put them in the washing machine, take them out, hang them up to dry, fold them up, put them away…

That's a long list of related vocabulary just from the noun *trousers*, and they are all common words.

Don't know a word? Write it down, check it online and practise it.

That was just an example. As with everything that you learn, put an emphasis on the vocabulary and grammar that you either want to learn or need to learn. You decide what you learn. That means that you should choose vocabulary related to whatever is relevant to you. If you work in a clothes shop, then maybe the example of trousers is relevant to you. If you don't or have no interest in clothes vocabulary, choose something else.

Day 18

If you need vocabulary related to business, how about words related to *email* or *meeting*?

> **THE BEST PLACE TO FIND RELEVANT VOCABULARY IS IN YOUR FLUENCY PRACTICE.**

Words and phrases that you want to say but you don't know how.

After you identify relevant vocabulary to learn, now you need to practise it. Remember, it's only by practising and playing with the words that you will be able to use them again in the future. Without practice, your brain will not consider the vocabulary important and you will forget it.

You don't learn vocabulary by looking at words in a dictionary. You learn vocabulary by using it.

To practise, make sentences with those words. Connect multiple words in a sentence. Ask questions using some of the words. Create a few negative sentences, conditionals and a variety of tenses.

The more you manipulate the vocabulary that you want to learn, the easier it will be to remember it.

So choose a word, idea or situation, and find as many related words as possible. Use a dictionary to find those words that you don't know. When you have a list, go through the words and decide which five words are most relevant to you.

Practise those words by playing with them, manipulating them or using them in any of the other drills that I have shown you.

Learn five words every day.

Which five words?

The words which you consider most relevant to you.

In one month, you will learn one hundred and fifty relevant words.

That's not a bad start.

REVIEW

- *What specific words and expressions do you think you should learn?*
- *When you speak in English, do you often get stuck trying to find the correct word?*
- *If so, which vocabulary do you have problems using?*
- *How much vocabulary do you identify when you do your daily fluency practice?*
- *How can you increase the number of words you learn during fluency practice?*

From tomorrow onwards, you will start doing fluency practice three times per day. Write them in your practice plan now.

Plan

Practise

Review

Reward

Do you want more practice? You can find an additional activity to practise the strategies from today's chapter in the free workbook. Visit www.how-to-english.com/workbook

DAY 19

HOW TO UNDERSTAND AND USE GRAMMAR CORRECTLY

"Don't learn grammar rules. Learn grammar situations."

"Children's brains are like sponges! It's easy for them to learn."

"My older brain is full of information, so it's harder for me to learn and remember language."

"I'm not a child anymore, so I can't learn languages very well."

We use children as an excuse for why we feel that we can't learn as adults. This is one of the biggest mistakes an adult learner can make.

It is true that you can only learn certain aspects of a language while the brain is still developing. For most people, perfect pronunciation, intonation and other aspects related to the "music" of the language need to be learned while the brain is still growing.

> **EVERYTHING ELSE IS YOURS TO LEARN.**

People just accept the sponge analogy as truth and think that they cannot learn. The sponge analogy is only that: an analogy. It's a comparison, but it's not an accurate comparison.

And it's not true.

The second excuse is absolute rubbish.

You can never fill the brain with information. You can never max out your brain's hard drive. The brain's learning capacity is almost limitless.

In fact, the opposite is true. The more you learn, the easier it is to learn and the healthier the brain becomes.

Removing these misconceptions is one of the best things you can do to help you make progress.

However, children do learn in a different way, but we should learn from them, instead of using them as an excuse for not learning.

Nobody asks why it is that children learn so well.

When you take a moment to analyse children's brains and look at how they learn, you see some very interesting things. Then, you can steal their tricks and use them to help you learn.

Great!

SO WHAT IS IT THAT CHILDREN DO THAT HELPS THEM TO LEARN LANGUAGES?

It's not that they are more intelligent than adults. After all, their brains are smaller. The tricks they use to learn languages so well are, in fact, very simple.

Adults overcomplicate everything.

Really, it is the way children behave and the way that they think that have the biggest impact on their ability to learn.

Children do four very important things that give them the upper hand in language learning.

> **THEY OBSERVE, LISTEN, COPY AND REPEAT.**

They are also very persistent (if you have children, you know what I'm talking about).

Let's break down those four things.

First of all, children observe. They observe everything, and they want to learn from everything.

Actually, that's not exactly correct.

It's not that they want to learn. They are just curious. Very curious. And curiosity leads directly to learning.

There's a difference.

They know that they don't know, but they are curious, and they want to know. So they go and find out.

As a result, they learn.

HOW DOES THIS WORK WITH LANGUAGE?

Well, they observe and remember situations, and they listen to what language is used in those situations. Then they copy and repeat the same words when they find themselves in a similar situation.

Observe, listen, copy and repeat.

Babies learn individual words this way.

"Daddy says 'bath' every time he puts me in this lovely, warm water."

They learn that the place where lovely, warm water is is the bath. The situation and context tell them this.

As they grow, they start to learn groups of words and phrases. You can see how they do this when they make a mistake with it.

Children learn the meaning of "we need to change the batteries" when something stops doing what it is supposed to do. A toy car stops moving and Mummy says, "We need to change the batteries."

I remember when the toilet in my house wouldn't flush, and my eldest son, who was two years old at the time, offered me some great advice: "Daddy, we need to change the batteries".

Hmm…not exactly.

The logic is there, but the context isn't exactly correct.

CHILDREN DO NOT LEARN GRAMMAR RULES.

They learn and remember situations and context. They observe situations and remember the language that is used in those situations.

But we don't teach language learners to be observant. We teach them grammar rules.

What are grammar rules and why do we teach them?

A grammar rule is basically an extremely compressed version of context and situation. It's a quick way of explaining the meaning of a tense, for example, without needing to show the learner multiple contexts over time that demonstrate the meaning.

It's a quick way to understand the concept of a tense without observing it "in action".

And that's great. It makes understanding it quick and easy.

The problem is that it doesn't help you use grammar. If you're in a conversation and you need to use a particular tense, you don't (and you can't) go through all the grammar rules in your head, then decide which tense is correct for the sentence that you want to say.

It takes too long.

Grammar rules are fantastic to understand the meaning of grammar.

But they are useless when you need to use grammar.

It's easier to remember and apply situation and context than it is to remember and apply grammar rules.

And this is exactly why children do this.

Because it's easier.

Day 19

And it works.

When you associate grammar with situations and context, and not rules, the correct verb tense simply "sounds right".

After all, this is how you do it in your own language. I imagine that you probably cannot explain the rules related to grammar in your language, but you can use them perfectly. The correct form just sounds right.

It sounds right because your brain can remember situations in which you heard the correct form. But your brain cannot remember any situations in which you heard the incorrect form. So the correct one just sounds right.

It's true that it takes longer to understand the meaning using the way that children learn. But when children finally learn the meaning, they learn it forever, and they are able to actually use it.

The child way makes it a little slow to understand grammar, but very easy to use.

The adult way makes it quick to understand grammar, but difficult to use.

WHICH ONE WOULD YOU PREFER?

Absolutely everything you need in a language you can learn from observing and listening.

The natural way of learning grammar is much better and gives far better long-term results.

This is how humans learn languages. It is the only way the brain knows how to learn languages. So you should learn English in a way that is natural and easy for you.

Observe, listen, copy and repeat.

PRACTICE
HOW TO MASTER QUESTION TAGS

"The easy way looks tempting, but the easy way will get you nowhere."

There are a few aspects of the English language that many learners try to avoid for as long as possible. An example of this is question tags.

Can you live without them?

Well, yes, you can.

Can you make good progress without them?

No, absolutely not.

All native speakers use question tags every day. If making progress is sounding more and more like a native speaker, then you absolutely cannot live without them.

So why do English learners avoid them if native speakers use them so regularly?

The answer is because, on the surface at least, they seem difficult.

And the sad truth is that people often avoid difficult things. People prefer anything which seems easier.

The problem is, easy will get you nowhere.

You can make massive progress if you take the challenge of learning something that at first seems like a challenge. When you become familiar with it, you suddenly find that your level jumps up, and your understanding of English improves.

EMBRACE EVERYTHING THAT SEEMS CHALLENGING, BECAUSE CHALLENGES BRING THE BEST REWARDS.

Day 19

The first step you can take is by learning and mastering question tags.

So what is a question tag, you ask?

A question tag is something that you put on the end of a sentence to make it a question.

Why do you want to make it a question?

The function of a question tag is to encourage a response from the listener, to confirm something that you already know or suspect, or to emphasise your statement.

Learning English is great, isn't it?

You're American, aren't you?

She hasn't been here before, has she?

A typical mistake that English learners make is to end a statement in English with *", no?"*, and to add more intonation.

We don't normally use this in English, so it can sound a bit strange.

We use question tags.

Let me ask you a question. How many times do you use the equivalent of a question tag in your language every day?

Lots.

And how many times do you use question tags when you speak English?

I'm guessing close to zero.

Do you see what I am trying to say here?

You need to finally learn and master question tags, once and for all.

"But they aren't easy to use, Adam. I have to think a lot!"

EASY WILL GET YOU NOWHERE. AND THINKING IS GOOD.

Here's how you learn and practise them.

The basic structure is this. If the sentence is affirmative, then the question tag is negative. If the sentence is negative, then the question tag is affirmative.

Positive, negative.

Negative, positive.

Yin and yang.

The perfect balance.

You make the question tag in the following way: auxiliary verb + subject.

You're American, aren't you?

She hasn't been here before, has she?

The only exceptions to this rule are the following:

*I'm late, **aren't** I?*

*Let's go, **shall** we?*

That's all you need to remember. Now you just need to apply it to a sentence.

You don't need a teacher next to you to tell you if you are using it correctly. You have the correct structure above so you can check it against your sentence and ask yourself if it's correct. If you know the tenses and their corresponding auxiliary verbs, you shouldn't have a problem with this.

NOW YOU NEED TO PRACTISE.

The first thing you can do is write a long list of very short sentences that contain a subject, verb and object. Don't write the question tag just yet.

They don't like dogs, …

Day 19

Adam loves running, …

You can't swim, …

It won't rain tomorrow, …

You're learning to play the piano, …

And so on…

Write around thirty short sentences like the ones above but without the question tags.

Then you read the sentences out loud and add the question tag as you say each one. You want to repeat the list until you can say the question tag without pausing and without thinking.

Remember, there shouldn't be a pause between the sentence and the question tag. If you pause, the question has a different meaning.

Repeat until there is no pause, and the sentence and question tag flow together.

When you can do that, change the list for another one and repeat.

It's simple and extremely effective. You can even have the list next to your computer monitor at work and practise a little throughout the day. You can write the correct question tag on a separate sheet of paper and check each answer in the beginning.

Another thing you can do is the following:

Take some text in English. A news article online is a good option. As you read the article, I want you to take every *subject + verb + object* in every sentence and add a question tag to it.

Don't worry if the sentence sounds strange. It's not important. What we're trying to do here is get the question tag to come out naturally. The text simply gives you a subject, verb and object for you to use as a base.

Let's take the paragraph above that starts with "You don't need a teacher next to you…" as an example. Now let's make question tags from the sentences in that paragraph.

You don't need a teacher next to you, do you?

You have the correct structure above, don't you?

You can check it against your sentence, can't you?

You shouldn't have a problem with this, should you?

You can do this with any text that has a subject, verb and object in it to practise question tags.

PRACTICE MAKES PERMANENT.

What is extremely important is that you say the question tags out loud. Remember, it's not what you practise, but how you practise that's important. If you practise writing question tags, you get good at writing question tags. The problem is, we mostly use question tags when we speak. You can write a million question tags, but if you can't say them, it's all for nothing.

Say them out loud.

When you get good at using question tags, everything else becomes much easier. You will be able to identify the tense, auxiliary verb and subject instantly and without thinking. You will sound much more natural, you will get extremely good at grammar and you will find that you start making progress again.

And you want to make progress, don't you?

Day 19

REVIEW

- *Do you pay attention to situation and context when learning grammar?*
- *How can you start to observe situation and context instead of grammar rules?*
- *How often do you use question tags?*
- *Do you think you make many mistakes with them?*
- *Would you like to be able to use them perfectly?*

Plan

Practise

Review

Reward

Do you want more practice? You can find an additional activity to practise the strategies from today's chapter in the free workbook. Visit www.how-to-english.com/workbook

DAY 20

HOW TO HAVE PERFECT GRAMMAR

*"Feed your brain what it likes to eat.
Everything else it will spit out."*

There's no avoiding it. You can't live without grammar.

Grammar is the glue that holds the language together, like the mortar that holds the bricks of a house together.

Without the mortar, the house falls apart.

Without grammar, language falls apart.

But it's very important to learn the right grammar. Relevant grammar.

Grammar is slightly different from vocabulary in the sense that of the hundreds of thousands of words in English, you will only need to learn a fraction of them.

However, all grammar is relevant. At some point, you will use all the grammar in the English language. But that doesn't mean you should practise all grammar all the time.

WHAT GRAMMAR SHOULD YOU PRACTISE?

The grammar that you have the most problems with.

Imagine you are building a house. A house of English. The words are the bricks of the house and the grammar is the mortar that keeps the bricks in place correctly.

If you have no problems with grammar, your house will be strong and everything will be in the correct place. But because you are learning

English, the chances are that there will be cracks in the walls of your house and mortar missing between bricks.

It's your job to identify those imperfections in your English and work to make your house stronger.

The main purpose of the fluency practice is to identify relevant vocabulary to learn, and to identify language and grammar that you make mistakes with or do not understand perfectly. By applying the techniques we covered in Part 2, you can identify specific grammar that you need to learn and practise. When you identify which grammar you have problems with, you can work to perfect it and make your house better and stronger.

Here is what you need to do to be able to use a grammar point perfectly: understand the grammar, then practise it until you can use it without hesitation or mistakes.

If you don't do both, you will not be able to use the grammar.

Yesterday, we saw that to truly understand grammar, the focus needs to be on observing situation and context, and seeing what language is used in that situation.

Feed your brain what it likes to eat. Everything else it will spit out.

FEED YOUR BRAIN SITUATION AND CONTEXT, NOT GRAMMAR RULES.

The next thing you need to do is practise. Not all practice is the same. It's not what you practise, but how you practise that is important.

There is a big problem with how grammar is typically practised in the classroom.

First, the teacher will explain the grammar point to the best of their ability with grammar rules and explanations. Then, they will normally

Day 20

practise the grammar point in a controlled way with some practice exercises, like gap-fill sentences or connecting sentence halves.

The problems come when the student leaves the classroom and enters the real world. Because the student received an explanation and did some practice, they think they now know the grammar. But when the student is in a situation where they need to use the grammar, they discover that they are unable to use it.

There are two problems that caused this. They lacked situation and context in the explanation of the grammar, and they didn't do enough practice. The practice that you normally do in the classroom generally isn't enough for you to be able to use the grammar perfectly in the real world.

To be able to use a grammar point perfectly, you need to practise it by speaking until you can use it without any mistakes at all. You also need to repeat the practice daily to give the brain time to absorb this new information.

It's not enough to only do some practice exercises in the classroom. You need to use the grammar in spoken form many times in order to perfect it. You need to produce the words, say the sentences and use it to really learn it well.

I understand why they generally don't do this in the classroom. Firstly, there just isn't enough time in a standard English class to do this. On top of this, there are usually many students in the classroom and each student cannot each have that amount of practice. The best the teacher can do is go around the class, asking each student in turn to use the grammar correctly, then give them some homework. And the problem with the homework is that it tends to be in written form, not spoken. You may be able to write it well, but if you don't practise by speaking, you won't be able to use it in a conversation.

So you can see that the classroom isn't the best place to practise grammar to perfection.

The classroom is a great place to get an explanation of a grammar point, but it can't help you very much with the practice part of perfecting grammar.

That means that it's your responsibility to practise on your own in order to make your grammar perfect.

As I always say, it's not what you do in class that determines your progress, it's what you do when you are not in class.

But that's great news!

It means that you have full control over your learning. You don't need to depend on another person to perfect your English grammar. You can depend on yourself.

Today, I'll show you how you can practise to perfection so that everything you learn, you learn perfectly and permanently.

Day 20

PRACTICE

HOW TO PRACTISE GRAMMAR CORRECTLY

*"If you do gap-fill exercises,
you get good at doing gap-fill exercises."*

I want to show you how to practise grammar to perfection using conditionals.

I want to show you with conditionals because they cause so many problems for English learners. Normally, when a teacher tells their students that they are going to study conditionals, everybody moans and complains. Everybody hates them.

Why do they hate them so much?

Because they have had lots of classes on conditionals and still cannot use them correctly. They are frustrated. And it's no wonder.

Think of how many classes you've had in English on conditionals. Five…ten…fifteen? But you still can't use them correctly.

I'm not surprised people don't like them.

Think about that for a moment. Five, ten, fifteen classes on conditionals, and most learners still can't use them. We can interpret this in two ways: either English learners all have a common flaw, or we're teaching them in the wrong way.

I think it was Einstein who once said, "Insanity is doing the same thing over and over, and expecting a different result each time."

The standard teaching methodology for conditionals is insane.

They do it once, it doesn't work. They do it again; still doesn't work.

Surely the logical thing would be to take a moment here to reconsider the tactics. But no, they do it another ten times, hoping the result will be different.

The only result is traumatised adults that cannot use conditionals correctly in a conversation. Well done!

The intentions aren't bad. They really want you to improve your use of conditionals. The only way they know how, though, is with these silly little gap-fill exercises, or match the two sentence halves, or…"yawn". The result is they can use them correctly in the classroom but not in the real world.

If you can use grammar in the classroom but not in the real world, that means you cannot use it well.

Again, it's not the teacher's fault. Most teachers and language schools only work with their students for the duration of the course. When the students finish the course, they never see them again. That means that they have no idea about how their methods work in the long term. I'm much more interested in long-term learning. I want my students to be able to use English not only now, but also into the future. Using English correctly now means nothing if you will forget most of it in a year.

THE MOST IMPORTANT THING IS NOT WHAT YOU LEARN, BUT HOW YOU LEARN. THAT IS WHAT WILL GIVE YOU LONG-TERM SUCCESS IN ENGLISH.

Why is this?

As a learner, you need to be very selective about *how* you practise because, in essence, you get good at how you practise, and not what you practise.

If you practise conditionals with gap-fill exercises, you get good at how you practise, and not what you practise.

Day 20

So what happens is that students get good at writing them, at putting the verb in the correct form into the little gap, and may even feel that they know how to use them. But then in a conversation, they will use them incorrectly.

When do you need to use conditionals? When you're speaking in English.

When do you make mistakes with conditionals? When you're speaking in English.

So, how do you need to practise conditionals? By speaking and saying them out loud.

I figured this out while learning Spanish. While reading my first book in Spanish, I saw a verb tense that I had never seen before. I had no idea what it is was so I went online to look it up. It turned out to be the verb tense that is used in second conditionals in Spanish.

At first, I was completely shocked that I had never seen or heard this tense before. Then I realised that the brain only sees what it wants to see and only hears what it wants to hear. I had seen and heard it before, but I had not paid any attention to it. I was only interested in getting the general understanding.

> **IF YOUR ONLY OBJECTIVE IS TO GET THE GENERAL UNDERSTANDING, THAT IS ALL YOU GET.**

Nothing more.

I was also surprised that I had been using conditionals incorrectly for a whole year and nobody had ever corrected me.

This is another misconception that people have about learning a language in a country where they speak your target language. Nobody is going to correct you, so you had better learn to correct yourself.

I realised that if I wanted to use conditionals correctly, I had to do something about it.

So I did the following practice exercise to perfect my use of conditionals.

I want you to do the same practice exercise to get a feel for how you should practise grammar.

Now I'm not going to go through the rules, explanations and all the rest, as I'm sure you've learned them many times already. I'm going to show you how to practise them.

Conditionals follow a fixed grammatical structure:

First conditional: *if + present, future*

Second conditional: *if + past simple, would + infinitive without to*

Third conditional: *if + past perfect, would + present perfect*

There are other ways of using conditionals, but for the purpose of this exercise, let's stick with the basics.

Write these structures down on a piece of paper.

Now sit on a chair in a comfortable place, and brace yourself for an hour of fun.

Say fifty first conditionals. Yes, fifty. Say them out loud, and check that what you say coincides with the written structure. You don't need a teacher to correct you here; you can correct yourself if you have the structure written down.

After twenty, you will feel a bit more confident, and won't need to check the structure. After thirty, you will get faster. And after forty, the words will flow off your tongue.

Now say fifty second conditionals.

"What? Again?!"

Oh yes. No pain, no gain.

Don't worry. You will be a machine by the end of the hour.

Day 20

After fifty second conditionals, say fifty third conditionals out loud. It doesn't matter what you choose to say in the conditionals that you create. You can make them as crazy as you like. The important thing is the grammar.

The difficult thing won't be the grammar but rather thinking of a conditional sentence. To help you with this, you can take the second part of your conditional sentence and use it as the first half of your next conditional sentence.

Here's an example.

"If I won the lottery, I'd buy a yacht. If I bought a yacht, I'd go out to sea every day. If I went out to sea every day, I'd see lots of sea life."

And so on…

In total, it should take around an hour.

Is it a pleasant hour? No, not really. It's certainly not your first choice for a Saturday evening. But what's great is that at the end of the hour, you will be completely cured of your mistakes, and you will be able to use conditionals perfectly at will.

YOU WILL FEEL GREAT.

You can, of course, choose not to do this activity. You can choose to spend probably the rest of your life having conditional classes in English.

Or one hour of intense practice.

YOU CHOOSE.

If you do this exercise, you will never make a mistake again with conditionals.

Find one hour over the next week to do this exercise and write it down in your practice plan and become awesome at conditionals.

From doing this exercise you will eliminate any mistakes you may be making with conditionals. More importantly, you will start to get an idea of *how* you need to practise grammar in the future in order to perfect it and use it without mistakes.

When you learn *how* to practise, you don't need to worry about *what* you practise.

REVIEW

- *How many mistakes have you identified since starting this book?*
- *What aspects of grammar do you have the most problems with?*
- *How many have you corrected?*
- *Are you comfortable using conditionals in English?*
- *What aspect of grammar do you most dislike and why?*
- *What would need to happen for you to like it?*

Plan: What, when and how you are going to practise.

Practise: Have good quality contact with English.

Review: Think about what you have learned today, what you have improved and what could be better.

Reward: Congratulate yourself and think about your achievements so far.

> Do you want more practice? You can find an additional activity to practise the strategies from today's chapter in the free workbook.
> Visit www.how-to-english.com/workbook

DAY 21

HOW TO IMPROVE YOUR PRONUNCIATION IN ENGLISH

"To speak well, you must listen well."

Listening practice is the perfect time to practise pronunciation.

I always teach listening and pronunciation together. Most teachers teach them separately or teach pronunciation with speaking.

I think this is a mistake.

The most important thing, without question, when practising pronunciation is to listen carefully. The only way you are able to pronounce correctly is if you are listening extremely carefully to the sounds that you hear and the sounds that you say.

You listen, then you repeat.

Listening and pronunciation are part of the same thing.

They are both related to sounds. One deals with receiving the sounds and the other deals with reproducing those sounds.

Many English learners get frustrated when trying to pronounce correctly. Difficult aspects of pronunciation like vowel sounds, consonant sounds, diphthongs and intonation can cause problems with adult learners.

When I teach pronunciation to adults, my aim is not to get the students to pronounce these sounds perfectly. I want them to pronounce as well as they can, but I don't obsess over perfection.

Excellence over perfection.

My aim is rather to get my students to hear the sounds, recognise them and be aware of their existence. My aim is to teach their ear to listen perfectly, not their mouth to pronounce perfectly.

With children, it's different.

We now know that in general, perfect pronunciation can only be achieved when the brain is developing.

> **CHILDREN CAN LEARN TO PRONOUNCE PERFECTLY, ADULTS CANNOT.**

There will be exceptions, of course, but in all my years teaching students from all over the world, I've never come across anybody that has learned perfect pronunciation as an adult.

I have taught many that had excellent pronunciation, some with nearly perfect pronunciation, but you could always tell that they were non-native speakers.

I speak French without any accent at all.

Why?

Because I moved there when I was twelve.

After a year, I was speaking French like any of the other French kids in my school, with no trace of an English accent.

When I moved to Spain aged twenty-seven and learned the language, I tried to develop the accent and found it impossible.

I could hear the sounds, but I was incapable of reproducing them perfectly. Even now, I still have an accent. Not an extremely strong one, but an accent nonetheless.

And I will always have an accent.

Day 21

And that's OK.

I'm not a child anymore, and reproducing perfect pronunciation in another language is almost impossible.

And if it isn't impossible, it requires hours and hours of dedicated work to be able to reproduce the sounds and incorporate them into your speech.

I recommend using this time to learn and practise other things.

Get as close as you can to perfect pronunciation without compromising other parts of speech.

> **AIM TO HAVE GOOD PRONUNCIATION, NOT PERFECT PRONUNCIATION.**

But what is possible - and extremely important - is to hear correct pronunciation; to hear and recognise regional accents; to hear intonation and its subtle differences in meaning when used in one way or another.

When I teach pronunciation to my adult learners, what am I really teaching them?

I'm teaching them to listen to these elements of pronunciation.

To listen to the sounds of the language.

To listen.

If you can learn to hear these things, then you develop fantastic listening skills.

> **PRONUNCIATION STARTS WITH LISTENING.**

What is the real purpose of pronunciation?

First of all, I will tell you what it isn't. It's not about having a perfect accent, which is what many people think. Never worry about that. If you're learning English as an adult, you will always have an accent. Foreign accents sound nice in English, so never feel embarrassed about the fact that you have one.

That is not the purpose of pronunciation.

THE REAL PURPOSE OF PRONUNCIATION IS COMPREHENSION.

Comprehension goes both ways. It is about people understanding you when you speak and you understanding others when they speak.

When teaching a child pronunciation, the focus is on producing perfect pronunciation as it is the only time in their life they will be able to do it.

With an adult learner, the focus should be on understanding others, being understood and listening to the sound of perfect pronunciation.

Here are a couple of ways that you practise pronunciation through listening.

After you finish and check your dictation on TED, take a look at the transcript. You will see that when you put the cursor over a sentence, the sentence lights up. If you click on that sentence, it will take you to the part of the video where the speaker says that sentence.

If you want to listen again, just click the sentence again.

The great thing about speaking in public is that the speakers exaggerate many aspects of pronunciation like sentence stress, word stress and intonation. They do this so their talk has more impact.

This is what you are going to listen for.

Click on a sentence and hear how the speaker says it. First, listen to the individual sounds that make up each word. Do you pronounce them in the same way? Practise and copy how the speaker says them. Then listen to the intonation and repeat with the same intonation. Then listen one last time. What about sentences stress? Try to repeat it. Try to hear which parts of pronunciation you have problems with.

Day 21

LISTEN, COPY AND REPEAT.

Another way to do this is to watch young children's programmes.

Children are much more aware of the sounds of the language than adults.

When you watch children's programmes, the intonation, sentence stress and word stress is much more exaggerated, because children react more strongly to these aspects of pronunciation than adults. This also makes it easier for English language learners to hear them.

Listen and repeat as close as you can to the original sentence. And don't worry, you won't end up speaking like a child.

It will just make you much more aware of these important parts of language, and slowly, they will make their way into your own speech, and you will sound much more natural.

Pronunciation is paramount for comprehension. The problem is, pronunciation classes tend to be boring and they are only taught in the classroom. Teachers rarely teach English learners how to listen to these elements of language on their own.

As a result, they never really learn and master pronunciation.

Now you know what to do every time you hear native English speakers speak.

Just listen, copy and repeat.

PRACTICE

HOW TO MASTER AUXILIARY VERBS (PART 1)

"A chain is as strong as its weakest link."

This is the first part in a series of three drills on auxiliary verbs.

Auxiliary verbs practice is a very powerful thing and the best way to practice and perfect your use of English grammar.

When English learners say they have problems using tenses or they make mistakes with grammatical structures, what they are really saying is that they make mistakes with auxiliary verbs when they speak English. Most mistakes with grammar tenses are mistakes with the use of auxiliary verbs.

If you take a sentence in any tense in English, the structure of the verb is almost always extremely easy to remember and use. In any tense, the verb will have one of only four different structures.

Let's take the verb *talk* as an example. The verb itself in all tenses takes one of the following forms: *talk, talks, talked* or *talking*.

So why do English learners make structural mistakes with tenses if the verb only takes a few forms?

The answer is that the most important structural aspects of a tense are auxiliary verbs, not the verb itself.

Do *you talk to your friends every day?*

I've been talking to my wife about the book.

He's talking to his boss.

Obviously, you need to remember which form of the verb to use. That goes without saying. You should also have a solid understanding of irregular verbs. In the case of irregular verbs, there are five verb forms instead of four. At intermediate or above (which you are), your knowledge of irregular verbs should be perfect, so that shouldn't cause you any problem. But the focus when practising verb tenses should be on perfecting your use of auxiliary verbs, not the form of the verb itself.

There are a few great ways to practise this. On Day 19 we looked at how regularly practising and using questions tags can help you do this. Starting today and over the next week I will give you three other simple ways to practise them, so you can finally consolidate your knowledge of auxiliary verbs and start using them without mistakes.

Mastering auxiliary verbs takes you one step closer to sounding like a native speaker and is the one thing that gives you perfect use of grammar.

Sound good?

Then let's start.

The first drill we will look at is using auxiliary verbs to show agreement with a speaker. You probably already do this by using the phrases *"Me too"* and *"Me neither"*.

I like going to the cinema.

- Me too.

I've never been to Austria.

- Me neither.

It's OK to use these phrases, but I recommend using the more challenging versions, *"So do I"* or *"Neither have I"*.

The structure you use is **so + auxiliary verb + subject** in the affirmative, and **neither + auxiliary verb + subject** in the negative.

The problem with *me too* and *me neither* is that you always give the same answer. The versions with *so* and *neither* require you to think a little more and analyse the sentence on a deeper level.

Is it more difficult?

Yes, a little. But as you now know, that which appears more difficult gives the best results.

Now you're probably thinking what most of my students think when I show them these structures: "I already know this, Adam. It's easy."

Then I ask those same students to respond to a variety of sentences using these structures and they generally need to think for a few seconds before giving the correct - or not - answer.

If you need to think for more than half a second to give the correct answer, it means that your use of auxiliary verbs is not perfect. With auxiliary verbs, anything other than perfect means you do not completely understand them well enough to be able to use them effectively.

You need to practise auxiliary verbs until you can provide the correct response perfectly and without pause or hesitation. If you cannot do that, then you should practise until you can.

You need to practise to perfection.

To do this, write a list of short and simple sentences. Each sentence must have a subject, verb and object, all in the first person and in a variety of tenses. When you have the list, you go through them responding with the correct structure. First in the affirmative, then in the negative.

Here's an example list of sentences in the affirmative.

I went to France last year.

I've visited three countries this year.

I'm learning to play the piano.

I'll probably go to the cinema at the weekend.

I have to go.

Take a minute to look at those sentences and come up with the correct response for each. Remember, the auxiliary verb changes depending on the tense.

Done?

You should have come up with the following responses:

So did I.

So have I.

So am I.

So will I.

So do I.

Then you practise agreeing in the negative by making each sentence negative.

I didn't go to France last year.

I haven't visited three countries this year.

I'm not learning to play the piano.

I probably won't go to the cinema at the weekend.

I don't have to go.

Now find the correct responses to agree in the negative.

You should have come up with the following responses:

Neither did I.

Neither have I.

Neither am I.

Neither will I.

Neither do I.

With practice, you will see that the amount of time you need to respond correctly will decrease. Use the same list until you can respond correctly and without hesitation. When you can do that, change the list for another and repeat. Do a little bit every day. You don't need to practise for more than five minutes per day with this.

With each list, you should also record yourself saying each sentence with a little pause between each one. Then, listen to each sentence and respond with the correct structure. That way you can practise as if it were a real conversation.

This is important because it is the closest you can get to a real conversation. This is the best way to practise as this structure is used almost exclusively in spoken English and informal conversations. In a conversation, you don't have the written form to help you and you need to rely on your listening skills. This adds another level of difficulty, but it is what will help you master it.

> **AS WITH ALL PRACTICE, YOU MUST SAY EACH SENTENCE OUT LOUD.**

Done correctly, auxiliary verb drills will provide you with everything you need to master grammar.

You have already learned all the rules and structural aspects of tenses. You don't need more of that. You need to practise using them and applying them in conversation. That is when most English learners make mistakes.

A chain is as strong as its weakest link. If there are weaknesses in your use of grammar, the chain will break at its weakest point. If you try to ignore these weaknesses, they will forever cause you problems.

To remove mistakes and master grammar, you need to practise what you most have difficulties with. When you confront those problems, they disappear.

Mastering your use of auxiliary verbs is the fastest way to do this.

Day 21

REVIEW

- *What sounds in English do you have difficulty pronouncing?*
- *How are you going to rectify that problem?*
- *How much attention do you pay to intonation?*
- *How long did it take you to think of and say the correct response in the auxiliary practice?*
- *Did you make many mistakes?*

Plan

Practise

Review

Reward

Do you want more practice? You can find an additional activity to practise the strategies from today's chapter in the free workbook. Visit www.how-to-english.com/workbook

DAY 22

HOW TO NEVER BE MISUNDERSTOOD WHEN SPEAKING IN ENGLISH

"A small change in how you learn can give massive results in what you learn."

In 2003, I went travelling in South America. My first stop was Quito, Ecuador. I went for a walk around the city on my first morning there. I saw a street vendor selling drinks on a corner. Feeling thirsty, I went and asked for a bottle of water. Here's how the conversation went.

"Hola. Agua, por favor"

"Qué?"

"Agua. Agua", and I started acting as if I were drinking water.

"Qué?", he repeated, with a confused look on his face. He obviously had no idea what I was talking about. The conversation continued exactly the same for a minute or so, until I pointed to a bottle of water and repeated the word.

"Ah...agua!", he said enthusiastically.

"That's what I've been saying all this time!", I thought. And it's true. I was saying the correct word, but there was something about the way I was pronouncing it that simply didn't make sense to him.

So often, people tell me stories of when they were in the UK or US, in a restaurant maybe, trying to order something that they knew they were pronouncing correctly, but no matter how many times they said it, the waiter just wouldn't understand them.

Has this happened to you? Frustrating, isn't it?

There's a technique that I teach my students which, if used correctly, consistently makes the listener understand you. When I teach this in class, I call the lesson "The number one tip for never being misunderstood in English".

It really does only require minimum effort and gives maximum results almost instantly.

Almost too easy.

I can tell you now that if you were pronouncing the word more or less correctly and the grammar was correct, I can almost guarantee that they didn't understand you because you weren't implementing this technique in English.

WHAT IS THE NUMBER ONE TIP FOR NEVER BEING MISUNDERSTOOD IN ENGLISH?

Emphasise the consonants.

Most pronunciation lessons in a typical English class tend to focus on the vowel sounds in English. I have come to realise that it's not the vowel sounds that cause these comprehension problems I just told you about. The comprehension problems are nearly always caused by mispronouncing the consonants.

Let me tell you a quick story. When I first arrived in Spain with my basic Spanish, one of the most difficult language skills for me was listening.

Everything just sounded like a long string of vowels, without any consonants. Spanish sounded something like this: uh-ah-ah-eh-ih-eh-oh-ah.

I remember when my wife said the word *washing machine* in Spanish (*lavadora*) in a conversation, and she literally had to repeat it ten times

Day 22

before I understood what she was trying to say to me.

All I could hear was ah-ah-oh-ah. I couldn't hear the consonants, only the vowels.

If you really listen to spoken English and really listen to the sound of the language, you'll notice that it's very consonant-heavy. The consonants sound strong.

Consonants in English are the most important sounds of the language. Not the most important letters, but the most important sounds. That's because the consonants in English are the sounds that carry the meaning of the word being said.

This means that if you're having a conversation with a native English speaker, their English-speaking brain will be subconsciously listening for the consonants, as it knows that these are the sounds that carry the meaning of the words.

Spanish, on the other hand, is the opposite. Their five vowel sounds are sacred, and they are always pronounced in the same way in all the Spanish-speaking world. Contrary to English, the vowel sounds in Spanish are the most important sounds.

As a result, consonants don't sound as strong in spoken Spanish, as it's the vowel sounds that carry the most meaning.

When my wife was saying *lavadora*, my English brain couldn't detect the consonants because they were weak compared to how they would be pronounced in English, so my brain couldn't detect the word.

This is why it was difficult for me to listen to and understand spoken Spanish when I first arrived in Spain.

The opposite happens when Spanish speakers travel to English-speaking countries. The consonants aren't strong when they speak, so English speakers will have difficulty understanding. And it's not only a problem for Spanish speakers. The same thing happens to speakers of most languages that don't have strong consonants.

If an English speaker can't hear the consonants clearly, they simply won't understand what you are saying.

To stop this from happening, all you need to do is make the consonants stronger. When I explain this, most people start speaking more loudly. That doesn't work, though.

It's not about speaking more loudly; it's about making the consonants stronger.

Make sure you are pronouncing each and every consonant that is supposed to be pronounced in a word. The consonants need to resonate.

This means that if the word ends in -ed, you should clearly pronounce the letter d, and it should resonate on the roof of your mouth. The -s in third person singular and plurals should be strong and clearly audible. There should be a clear difference in pronunciation between the letters v and b, the hard g and the c, and j and y. And each should sound strong and clear.

If you pronounce these pairs of letters in more or less the same way, people are going to misunderstand you.

IF YOU CAN PRODUCE EACH CONSONANT SOUND CLEARLY, NOBODY WILL MISUNDERSTAND YOU.

Guaranteed.

Here's how you can practise this.

Listen to some spoken English after reading this chapter and make a conscious effort to really listen to the sound of the language, paying attention to the sound of the consonants as the person speaks. Don't worry about understanding what the person is saying, that's not the exercise. Just listen to the sound of it, and listen to how the consonants resonate and sound strong.

Now try this. Take a paragraph of text in English. It can be anything, it doesn't matter. Read it slowly, unnaturally slowly, and make the consonants sound as strong as possible. It will sound unnatural, and that's OK. It's only practice. The idea is to get your brain to focus on the consonants more, and train the mouth and tongue to produce strong consonants. Really exaggerate them for this practice exercise and train the physicality of producing these sounds.

It will feel strange in the beginning as you've probably never paid any attention to these sounds before, but the more you practise, the easier it will feel, and you'll begin to adopt this pronunciation in normal conversation.

PRACTICE MAKES PERMANENT.

Another fantastic way to do this is by looking up words containing problematic consonants in an online dictionary, where you can hear these words pronounced in a variety of accents to hear how they are pronounced. You'll hear that the consonants resonate.

After a few days, you'll become much more aware of the sounds that you're making when you speak in English.

More importantly, you will never be misunderstood.

This is the key to speaking clearly in English.

PRACTICE

HOW TO MASTER AUXILIARY VERBS (PART 2)

"If something is challenging, it's probably worth doing."

Yesterday we looked at the power of auxiliary verbs to help you master your use of grammar and verb tenses.

The reason auxiliary verb practice is so powerful is that in order to use them correctly, you need to be able to identify the tense, the corresponding auxiliary verb, put it all in the correct order, then say it, all in much less than one second.

Yes, it really does need to be that quick. Anything slower and it won't sound natural and shows that you don't have complete control over it.

When you are able to complete all those brain processes almost instantly, it shows that you have incredible control over your use of English grammar.

It means that you are able to process English in your brain very quickly, and that skill helps you in all other aspects of your English.

It will be challenging in the beginning. However, if something is challenging, it probably means it's worth doing.

Yesterday we looked at how to use auxiliary verbs for agreement. Today we will cover disagreement to add another level of difficulty. When I say difficulty, what I mean is that it requires you to think a little more and process the information in a different way. And thinking is good.

The structure to disagree in the negative is *subject + negative auxiliary verb*

Day 22

Let's use the same sentences from yesterday to practise this.

I went to France last year.

I've visited three countries this year.

I'm learning to play the piano.

I'll probably go to the cinema at the weekend.

I have to go.

Imagine that these sentences are not true for you and you want to show disagreement. Respond to each using the structure above.

Have a think for a moment.

Done?

You should have come up with the following responses:

I didn't.

I haven't.

I'm not.

I won't.

I don't.

Now make each sentence negative and repeat, this time disagreeing in the affirmative.

I didn't go to France last year.

I haven't visited three countries this year.

I'm not learning to play the piano.

I probably won't go to the cinema at the weekend.

I don't have to go.

Take a moment to think of the correct response for each.

Done?

You should have come up with the following responses:

I did.

I have.

I am.

I will.

I do.

Just as you did for yesterday's drill, practise until you can respond correctly and without hesitation. When you can do that, change the sentences and repeat. Practise a few minutes, a few times per week until you can use them perfectly in conversation.

In two days, we will cover the last of the drills using auxiliary verbs. Auxiliary verb drills and question tags practice are all you need to solidify your use of grammar.

To perfect your *understanding* of grammar and verb tenses, all you need to do is pay more attention to situation and context.

To perfect your *use* of verb tenses, all you need to do is regular auxiliary verb drills.

I always try to teach what the absolute minimum is that you need to do to reach your goals. Doing the absolute minimum doesn't mean you do less. It means you can do more by doing only what is necessary. You eliminate those things which don't move you closer to your goal, and only do those things which move you closer.

IT'S NOT LAZY LEARNING, IT'S EFFICIENT LEARNING.

Observing situation and context plus regular auxiliary verb drills are the absolute minimum you need to do to master grammar and verb tenses.

Day 22

Perfect your understanding of grammar and perfect your use of grammar.

Perfect.

REVIEW

- *How many English activities do you have in your practice plan for this week?*
- *How many have you missed over the last week?*
- *Why did you miss them?*
- *What can you do to avoid missing them again?*
- *How does the auxiliary verb practice feel?*
- *How much time do you need to give the correct answer?*

Plan

Practise

Review

Reward

Do you want more practice? You can find an additional activity to practise the strategies from today's chapter in the free workbook.
Visit www.how-to-english.com/workbook

DAY 23

HOW TO IMPROVE YOUR MEMORY
REMEMBER EVERYTHING YOU LEARN IN ENGLISH

*"Memory is like a bottle of orange juice.
If you don't shake it up, it all settles at the bottom."*

In 2007, a man named Dave Farrow broke the world memory record for the most decks of cards memorised in a single sighting. 59 decks of cards to be precise. That's a total of 3,068 individual cards, which took him 14 hours to memorise, and 9 hours to recall.

That's a pretty incredible feat. I'd probably max out at ten, I think.

Ten cards, that is, not ten decks!

I wonder what would happen if you asked him now, years after this record was set, to recall the cards. How many would he be able to recall?

I doubt he would be able to recall the whole sequence, but I'm sure he would remember at least some.

Or maybe not…

He'd be using a totally different part of his memory to recall that sequence ten years after. His long-term memory would now be responsible for recalling those cards. The cards that he would recall now would be the ones that he has a "memory" of. A memory like the ones we have of our childhood holidays, for example.

And long-term memory lacks detail.

The way these memory champions perform these incredible feats is by training and stretching their short-term memory – which has limited capacity – via a variety of techniques to recall in perfect detail a random sequence of cards.

Long-term memory is almost limitless, but lacks detail. Short-term memory has incredible detail, but is quite limited.

Think of a computer. A standard computer has two types of memory: RAM and a hard drive. The computer uses RAM to "remember" information that it needs to use in the immediate future, and uses the hard drive for "storing" information in the long-term. RAM memory is relatively small, but the hard drive is much bigger.

Another key point with RAM memory is that when the information has been used for the task at hand, the information is deleted and lost.

Humans "delete" or lose information from our memory in a different way.

A psychologist called Hermann Ebbinghaus discovered the rate at which the brain forgets new information. He found that without the use of retention techniques, a person forgets 50% of what they learned after only a few hours. A day later, that same person will have forgotten 75% of the information. And after one week, 90% of the information will be lost.

That means that a week after you learn something, you will have forgotten 90% of it.

> **UNLESS YOU DO SOMETHING ABOUT IT.**

To find out what you can do to prevent this from happening, we need to take a look at what happens in the brain when you learn.

When you are exposed to some new information, a group of neurons fire together, creating a connection. To simplify this, let's call this connection a memory.

The more these neurons are stimulated, the more permanent the connection becomes. In other words, the more they are stimulated, the stronger the memory becomes. As the neuropsychologist Donald Hebb once said, "Neurons that fire together, wire together."

To keep new information in your memory, you just need to make sure those groups of neurons fire together as much as possible.

There are a few things that you can do to stimulate those connections and make them strong and easy to remember.

To have a good memory, all you need to do is maximise the amount of information that you remember, and minimise the amount of information that you forget.

Think of memory as creating connections in the brain and then stimulating those same connections repeatedly to prevent the connection from being lost. There are little tricks that you can use to stimulate the connections between neurons.

Things that favour stimulation and help memory are interest, comprehension, association, visualisation, context, dynamics and repetition.

When memory champions remember a sequence of cards, they use a number of these techniques, particularly visualisation, to create a visual story in their head. When they recall the sequence, they go through the story in their head, with each card having a place in the story.

That's fine for short-term memory, but with English learning, you need to use your long-term memory. The best way is to use a variety of these techniques to remember everything that you learn in English.

1. **Interest**

   When you are interested in what you learn, the amount of information that you remember increases dramatically. A friend of mine can remember every football match that was played in each of the world cups since 1982, including who won and the score. He loves football, so it's very easy for him to do this. In fact, he memorises it all almost automatically because he loves it so much.

   You probably have a similar talent for memorising information that you find interesting.

   Interest allows you to remember information without effort.

   How do you most enjoy learning English? What activities get your attention the most?

   Do more of those activities.

   Enjoying what you learn is the easiest way to maximise the amount of information you remember. The best way to do this is by taking an activity or hobby that you currently do and enjoy, and then do it in English. Do you enjoy watching films? Then watch films in English. Do you enjoy reading fashion magazines? Then read fashion magazines in English. Do you listen to podcasts about your hobbies and interests? Then listen to similar podcasts in English.

   Enjoy what you learn.

2. **Comprehension**

   This simply means that you understand the information that you learn. This makes sense as it's almost impossible to remember something that you don't understand.

   With everything that you learn in English, make sure you understand it completely and not just superficially.

   I like to give my students challenges. One of the challenges I often give them is to teach something to the class in English. But not just anything. They need to teach something related to an aspect of English, normally a verb tense or grammar point.

When you learn something with the intention of teaching it, you find that you learn it in a different way. You learn all the smaller details of it and leave nothing out.

Why?

Because you can't teach something that you don't completely understand.

With everything that you learn in English, learn everything there is to learn about it and you won't forget it.

3. Association

This means associating the information that you want to learn with something that you already know and understand. The simple way to do this is by finding the translation of the word into your own language.

You can go further and associate the word with the place that you first learned it or the person who taught it to you. Many people like to create a strange or memorable association between a word and what it reminds them of, for example, *ice cream* and *I scream*. Then they make a visualisation of a person screaming the word *ice cream*.

This technique works by connecting the word to a memory that you already have.

More connections, more memory.

4. Visualisation

This is related to association.

With each new word or phrase that you learn, you create an image of it in your head. The word is then connected to an image, and the brain likes images more than it likes words. Images have life, words do not.

Try to create an image of the situation that the word, phrase or grammar is used in.

5. Context

As we have already seen in other chapters, context is what gives meaning to language.

We use language in particular contexts and situations. This is true for both vocabulary and grammar. With everything you learn in English, focus on the situation and connect the language to the context that it is used in. Visualise it and visualise yourself using the language correctly in that situation.

Context gives life to language and is the key to really understanding it.

6. Dynamics

Dynamics means using and manipulating the information that you want to remember. To simplify, let's call it practice.

The more you practise and manipulate the information, the more you stimulate the connections and strengthen your memory of it. Don't only use it in one way. Use the language in multiple drills, like the ones I have shown you. Create new sentences with the word or phrase, then manipulate those sentences by changing a word, changing the tense, or making it negative or interrogative.

The more you play with the language, the more you will remember.

7. Repetition

Repetition is the classic way of learning individual words.

This is probably the way that you learned the list of irregular verbs in English. Unfortunately, the way they taught you to repeat words was lifeless and dry, and most people end up hating what they are trying to learn. If you don't enjoy what you learn, you will never remember it.

When I talk about repetition, I simply mean repetitive practice.

Imagine you learn ten new words in one day. It is essential that you do a little practice the following day to avoid forgetting the list. Practise the list with drills and these other techniques. A few days later, do the same and then again after a week. Here's another fantastic and easy way to repeat vocabulary. Write the words and expressions that you want to remember on post-its. Stick the post-its around the house and leave them there for a week or so. Every time you walk past a post-it, say it out loud in a short example sentence.

Day 23

This will drastically increase the amount you remember and minimise the amount that you will forget.

This is why it is so important to regularly practise everything you write in your notebook. If you don't practise what you learn, you will have more and more problems remembering that information until you can't remember it at all.

As with every learning technique, there will be some that give you great results and others that don't work so well for you. Your goal when trying these techniques is to identify which work best and which don't work so well for you. Do more practice with the techniques that work well, and do less with the ones that don't.

Hackers are able to access all the information on a computer by employing a variety of techniques.

If you employ these memory techniques, you can also hack the brain to maximise learning and access all the information you have in your memory.

HOW TO ENGLISH

PRACTICE

HOW TO EASILY REMEMBER LONG LISTS OF WORDS

"A little every day is far better than a lot one day."

Do you remember "cramming" for an exam at school or university? Everybody did it! How much information do you remember from that exam?

Probably very little, right?

By cramming (forcing things into a small place), we use our short-term memory. We do this because most people only care about remembering the information to pass the exam. As a result, when you finish the exam, your brain deletes the information.

> **HOW CAN YOU TRANSFER INFORMATION FROM SHORT-TERM TO LONG-TERM MEMORY?**

With our good friend *working memory*.

Working memory is responsible for the manipulation of information that is stored in the one and a half kilos of jelly inside the skull. And by *manipulating*, I mean *using*.

And that's where the common expression "use it or lose it" comes from.

The problem is that when we want to remember lists of vocabulary, like dependent prepositions or verbs that are followed by a gerund or an infinitive, many learners use this cramming technique.

Cramming is a bad technique to use if you want to remember information long-term.

Day 23

You now know the importance of language manipulation to help you remember English, and there's a simple exercise I recommend to easily remember long lists of vocabulary in English.

A technique I call passive memorisation.

With active memorisation, which is the classic technique language learners use, a student has a list of vocabulary and actively tries to memorise the list.

This doesn't work long-term, however, because the brain will recognise this information as something it needs now, and will activate the short-term memory, which is useless for remembering things long-term.

So here's what you do.

Take a list of vocabulary, for example dependent prepositions, which English learners often have problems with.

Now print the list out or save it on your laptop or mobile and have it near you for a week or so.

Read the list out loud, and make an example sentence with each verb and dependent preposition. A simple sentence, it doesn't matter.

By reading out loud and making example sentences, you're manipulating the information by reading it, saying it and using it in a sentence.

The more manipulation, the better. More neurons will be firing. Just as we saw in the main chapter, neurons that fire together, wire together.

Read them all out loud, but don't try to memorise them. Just read them out loud.

Do this in the morning. It takes no more than two minutes.

At lunchtime, read the list out loud again. Again, it will take no more than two minutes. Finally, repeat the exercise one more time in the evening, making a new sentence with each verb.

Do this every day for one week, and after one week, you will simply know which preposition is correct. It will just "sound" correct.

And this is how they sound to native speakers.

This is what you will achieve from doing this simple, zero-effort exercise.

The easiest way is sometimes the best way. And the key is a little bit every day. That is how you transfer the information to your long-term memory. With cramming, you only activate your short-term memory.

> **WITH ENGLISH LEARNING, A LITTLE EVERY DAY IS FAR BETTER THAN A LOT ONE DAY.**

The following week, find a new list and repeat the exercise. In a few months, you'll have remembered an incredible amount of new vocabulary.

Active memorisation requires a lot of effort and time in the short-term, but it only gives you short-term success.

Passive memorisation requires very little effort and time, gives no short-term success, but guarantees long-term success.

And long-term success is what really matters in mastering English.

Day 23

REVIEW

- *What things that interest you do you have no problem remembering?*
- *How you do you think you could apply that skill to English?*
- *Which memory technique do you think will work best for you?*
- *How often are you reading out loud?*
- *Which fluency drill works best for you so far?*

Plan

Practise

Review

Reward

Do you want more practice? You can find an additional activity to practise the strategies from today's chapter in the free workbook. Visit www.how-to-english.com/workbook

DAY 24

MOTIVATION, SELF-DISCIPLINE AND HABITS (PART 3)
HOW TO IMPROVE YOUR SELF-DISCIPLINE

"You can experience the minor pain of self-discipline now or the major pain of regret later."

I like to do little experiments on myself.

A few years ago, I went a whole year without any caffeine at all.

It was interesting.

The year after I started learning how to do freestanding handstands.

I like seeing how my body responds to each little experiment, and I learn something new with every one that I do. When I complete the time I set for each experiment, I decide if I want to continue doing it or not.

Some I continue doing because they give me some kind of benefit, and some I stop because they don't.

WHY DO I DO THESE EXPERIMENTS?

A big part of my job is telling people what to do. I tell people what to do to improve their English, how to be motivated, how to plan their goals in English learning and how to reach those goals. I know how difficult it can be to start and keep a new habit, so I start my own new habits in the form of experiments. That way I can experience exactly what my students experience when they take my advice.

I also like to take advice from others and try out new things that people recommend. I think that if I can't take other people's advice, I am not in a position to give advice.

A couple of years ago, for example, someone recommended I take cold showers. I tried it and I've been taking cold showers ever since.

This person's exact words were, "Adam, you have to have cold showers! They're great!"

So I did.

Let me be the first to tell you that cold showers are not great at all. If somebody ever tells you that, they're lying.

It is true that you feel great after the cold shower, but that doesn't mean that cold showers themselves feel great.

It's the same as if somebody were to slap you in the face repeatedly for two minutes. When they stop, it feels great. But the slapping isn't nice.

Cold showers are the same.

I still take cold showers, but I still don't enjoy them.

Why do I still take them even if I don't enjoy them?

I take them so I can practise one of two very important skills that are essential if you have a goal that you want to achieve.

THOSE TWO SKILLS ARE MOTIVATION AND SELF-DISCIPLINE.

We have already seen that motivation is something that promotes the desire or willingness to do or achieve something.

Discipline is what makes you act in accordance with rules. Self-discipline means to act in accordance with rules that you put in place for yourself.

Day 24

Motivation is very closely related to emotions, as it deals with the desire that you have to do a particular task.

Self-discipline, on the other hand, is unrelated to emotions. It means you do the task, whether you want to or not.

Two of the most common goals that people set themselves are losing weight and learning another language. Unfortunately, many people fail to achieve these goals. Others achieve one of their goals, but find that when they finish they start to put on weight again or lose the language level that they have reached.

WHY DO PEOPLE OFTEN FAIL TO ACHIEVE THEIR GOALS?

What's difficult is not the task itself but keeping the habit of watching what you eat and doing exercise, or practising the language on a daily basis, come rain or shine.

What's difficult is maintaining self-discipline, not the task itself.

There are distractions and temptations, and if you don't have the self-discipline to do what you need to, in spite of those distractions and temptations, then you fail.

It's that simple.

Let's imagine you want to take up running.

Here's a quick fact about running. When you first start, the first few runs are not nice at all.

They are horrible.

You feel ill, you feel as if your head is about to explode, your legs hurt and your lungs hurt.

So naturally, afterwards, your brain says, "No way! That's it. No more of that. We are never going to do that again!"

Only one of two things will get you out of that door again: motivation or discipline.

If your motivation is stronger than your desire to not run again, that will get you out the door.

If your motivation isn't stronger than your desire to not run again, then self-discipline will decide if you run again or not.

And if your self-discipline is stronger than your desire to not run, you will run.

If it isn't, you won't.

When you are faced with a task - any task - motivation will decide if you do it without thinking about it.

This is logical. If you want to do something, you just do it. You don't need to persuade yourself.

If there is no motivation (and let's be honest, sometimes, for whatever reason, we just don't feel like doing a particular task) then self-discipline will decide if you do it or not.

And this is where the internal battle between Good Intentions and Instant Gratification starts in your head as you try to persuade yourself to do it.

"I need to do it. I know, but I don't feel like it. I'll do it tomorrow instead. Well… it can't really wait till tomorrow. Then let's do it when this programme finishes. But I really need to do it now…but I can't be bothered…etc, etc, etc…"

This battle is between your desire for immediate pleasure and your desire for benefits in the future. Part of your brain wants to relax now and another part of your brain knows that if you do what you need to do, your future will be better.

WHO WINS THE BATTLE?

Well, just like any battle: the strongest or smartest one.

You can learn all the theory you want about the goal that you want to

Day 24

achieve, but if you don't have either motivation or self-discipline, you will fail.

Motivation is great, but you won't always feel motivated. And if there is no motivation (and sometimes there isn't and that's OK), then self-discipline is the only thing that will get you from A to B.

Improving your self-discipline is THE best thing you can do to help you achieve absolutely anything you want.

Motivation sounds good and it feels good. At some point though, you will need to rely on self-discipline.

Not a lot is out there on the subject of practising self-discipline.

Why not?

Well because it's not particularly sexy.

Self-discipline sounds boring.

Self-discipline means to do a task that will benefit you in the long term, but that you don't necessarily want to do in the present and that doesn't necessarily feel good. Then you do it again. And then again. And then... you get the idea.

There's not really a way to make that sound sexy or attractive.

Because it isn't.

There will be days when you don't feel like doing English practice. Those days are the perfect opportunity to practise and improve self-discipline. To become a self-discipline machine, you just make sure you do your English practice, whether you feel like it or not.

After, you will feel great and proud of yourself for not succumbing to your temptations to not do it.

Eventually - and this is the best bit - you actually start to enjoy it.

SELF-DISCIPLINE CREATES MOTIVATION.

To really improve self-discipline, practise it in other aspects of your life too, not only English. Maybe you could do fifty squats every day, or clean and tidy a different part of your house for fifteen minutes every day, or read twenty pages of a book.

It should be a task or activity that you don't normally do on a daily basis. It should also be something that is tempting not to do. And of course, it should be something that benefits you in the long term.

You force yourself to do it, even if you don't want to. You decide to do it, and you just do it.

Long story short, that's why I take cold showers.

I never look forward to it, and it feels horrible, but I feel good afterwards and my self-discipline has improved dramatically as a result.

WHY DO I NEED TO IMPROVE MY SELF-DISCIPLINE?

Because I want to help people.

I want to help frustrated English learners. And in order to do that, I have to write. But I'm not a writer by profession, so I had to force myself to do it when I started.

Before I started my blog, I had never written anything.

I went from zero to writing a few thousand words every week.

In the beginning, I did not feel like writing at all. I realised that I needed to train my self-discipline. The motivation wasn't strong enough to force me to sit down for hours to write.

After a while, I created a habit and I started to enjoy it.

Now I have motivation and don't need self-discipline for writing.

Self-discipline creates motivation.

If you're trying to improve your English, take a few minutes every day to practise self-discipline. It's the superpower that will get you to your goal, whatever obstacles come your way.

Day 24

Do you remember the English expression *"Slowly slowly catchy monkey"* from Day 16? This is the idea that in order to achieve your goal, you should plan and reach small milestones.

Well, it turns out that there is a simple technique you can employ to catch these fast and agile animals.

First, you take a jar that has a small opening in the top, just wide enough for a monkey to put its hand in. Then, tie the jar to a tree so the monkey cannot pick it up and carry it away. Finally, you place some food that monkeys like around the jar and a little inside the jar itself.

Eventually, a monkey will come and put its hand in the jar to take the food. But of course, it can't take its hand out of the jar without sacrificing the food. The monkey will not let go of the food. At this point, you can simply pick up the monkey and take it away.

The monkey will not sacrifice what it has in its hand.

Humans have the unique capability to make sacrifices in the present in order to guarantee a better future. Of course, it doesn't feel good to make that present sacrifice, but you can be sure that by making that sacrifice, you will benefit as a result.

Many people think that self-discipline is painful, but it's actually not.

SELF-DISCIPLINE IS FREEDOM.

Freedom from what?

Freedom from regret. Freedom from your frustrations. Freedom from present desires.

It gives you freedom to do what you know is good for you and what you really want to do. It gives you freedom to satisfy your long-term desires.

Freedom to achieve all your goals.

PRACTICE

HOW TO MASTER AUXILIARY VERBS (PART 3)

"Five minutes of focused activity is far better than two hours of half-hearted effort."

Welcome to the last installment of auxiliary verb drills.

In Part 1, I showed you how to practise auxiliary verbs to show agreement with another person. In Part 2, we covered how to practise showing disagreement.

Today, we will look at how to use them to express surprise. Then we will combine all the auxiliary verb drills we have looked at to create one drill to practise all of them.

Three drills in one.

To express surprise at what a speaker has said, you use the following simple interrogative structure:

AUXILIARY VERB + SUBJECT ?

Let's use the same short sentences from the previous drills to show you how this works.

I went to France last year.

I've visited three countries this year.

I'm learning to play the piano.

I'll probably go to the cinema at the weekend.

I have to go.

Day 24

Imagine someone you are speaking to says these sentences and you want to show surprise or interest, how do you respond correctly using the structure above?

Have a think for a moment.

Done?

You should have come up with the following responses:

Did you?

Have you?

Are you?

Will you?

Do you?

Ok, great. That shouldn't have caused you too much difficulty. Now in negative:

I didn't go to France last year.

I haven't visited three countries this year.

I'm not learning to play the piano.

I probably won't go to the cinema at the weekend.

I don't have to go.

Have a think for a moment.

Done?

You should have come up with the following responses:

Didn't you?

Haven't you?

Aren't you?

Won't you?

Don't you?

Fantastic. Now we are going to combine all three drills into one. You now need to show surprise, then either show agreement or disagreement, whichever one is true for you.

Here's what I would say as a response to each of the above affirmative sentences:

Did you? So did I.

Have you? I haven't.

Are you? So am I.

Will you? I probably won't.

Do you? So do I.

And here is what I would say as a response to each in the negative:

Didn't you? I did.

Haven't you? Neither have I.

Aren't you? I am.

Won't you? Neither will I.

Don't you? I do.

The best way to practise all three drills is to take a few simple sentences like these in the affirmative then do the following:

1. Show surprise then show agreement to all the sentences
2. Show surprise then show disagreement to all the sentences
3. Show surprise then say whichever response is true for you, either agreement or disagreement

Then make all the sentences negative and repeat. When you can give a response instantly, change the sentences and repeat. It takes a few minutes and no matter what your level is, you will need to practise this until it's perfect.

Day 24

When you understand grammar by observing situation and context, and you can use it correctly by doing these drills, that is when you have perfect grammar.

This is the best and fastest way to achieve it.

REVIEW

- *How self-disciplined are you, in your opinion?*
- *When do you find it easy to succumb to temptation?*
- *When do you feel least motivated to practise English?*
- *How do you think you could improve your self-discipline?*

Plan

Practise

Review

Reward

Do you want more practice? You can find an additional activity to practise the strategies from today's chapter in the free workbook. Visit www.how-to-english.com/workbook

PART IV

PLANNING FOR THE FUTURE: HOW TO BECOME AN INDEPENDENT ENGLISH LEARNER

"When others make decisions for you, your future depends on them. When you make your own decisions, you decide what your future will be."

DAY 25

HOW TO IMPROVE YOUR WEAKNESS
THE ONE THING THAT ENGLISH LEARNERS RARELY DO

"What you most avoid is what you most want and need."

It's almost impossible for humans to walk in a straight line.

Over a short distance, there should be no problem. And if you're following something, you should be fine too.

But over a long distance, the body tends to move towards one side and, slowly but surely, after a while you'll be completely off course. You may even complete a full circle.

One of the reasons for this is that we all have a dominant leg. This means that the other leg is slightly weaker.

When one leg is stronger than the other, this changes the way you walk ever so slightly, and without a reference point to walk towards, you end up walking in circles.

In sports and exercise, many injuries result from similar muscle imbalances, when one muscle or muscle group becomes stronger than its opposing muscle.

The sad thing is, we tend to put the blame on the dominant, stronger muscle. But really, we should be focusing on the weaker counterpart.

Is the problem the fact that one leg is stronger than the other, or that one leg is weaker than the other?

This happens in language learning too.

The majority of the practice that most English learners do is input, and very little output, which can be seen in this graph.

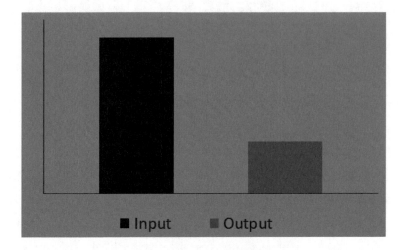

WHAT DOES THIS MEAN?

It means that most learners receive English by listening and reading, but rarely produce English by speaking.

Most learners complain that they find it hard to improve their speaking skills, and say that their comprehension skills are pretty good. The problem is, you get good at how you practise, not what you practise. If you only practise comprehension, you feel comfortable with comprehension. If you don't practise speaking very often, you don't feel comfortable speaking.

Think about your own learning for a moment.

Of all the hours of contact you have with English, how many do you spend listening and reading, and how many do you spend speaking?

Day 25

If I had to guess, I'd say around 90% reading and listening, and 10% speaking.

When you look at it like that, it's not very surprising that you find it difficult to speak fluently, but not so difficult to read or listen.

Just as a muscle imbalance in your body can stop you reaching your full potential in sports, an imbalance in language skills can slow your progress horribly.

If your fluency was as good as your listening or reading comprehension, would you be happy?

Probably, yes.

English learners need to think about how much contact they have with each skill, and adapt their practice plan accordingly.

In tennis, you can find players in the top 100 that have an extremely good and dominant strength, like a formidable serve. However, unless the other aspects of their game are similarly good, they will never reach the top 10.

The only players you find in the top 10 are the all-round great players.

You can be good at a skill by focusing on one or two aspects of that skill, but you can never be great. If you work on improving all aspects of a skill, you will be great.

How can you become a great, all-round English learner?

A large part of the contact you have with English needs to be producing English, practising what you know by speaking or doing productive listening practice, like dictations.

This is where most people go wrong. They spend huge amounts of time reading or listening for general understanding, but very little time producing any English.

I told you about the importance of fluency practice at the beginning of the book.

WHY AM I TELLING YOU THIS AGAIN?

Because, if I had to make a bet on which of the practice exercises you *haven't* been doing regularly, I would bet on the daily fluency practice. I know my students well. They know they should do it, and they know that it's the most important practice that they can do. But so often, they simply don't do it.

What you most avoid is what you most want and need. If you continue to avoid what you know is good for you, you will never get the results you want and deserve.

Why is it always this way? Why is it always easier to find time to practise listening and reading than it is to practise speaking?

The short answer is because it's incredibly easy to practise these skills with little or no effort.

You can literally sit on the sofa with your feet up doing nothing, and practise your reading or listening skills. All the information comes in. There's no need to produce anything.

All input, little output.

Tempting, isn't it?

It's much easier to allow language to come in than it is to produce language.

To listen or read you don't actually need to do anything or think that much. With speaking (and writing), you have to do something. It's not a lot, but when the brain has to choose between zero effort and some effort, it will always prefer to take the easy option.

However, easy doesn't often lead to much in life. Embrace what appears to be difficult, because that's where all the fantastic results are.

Day 25

As the old saying goes, "All the magic happens outside your comfort zone."

But the truth is, it's not even difficult to practise and improve your speaking. It only seems that way.

WHAT DO YOU NEED TO DO TO IMPROVE YOUR SPEAKING SKILLS?

Speak. It really is that simple.

Instead of spending 90% of the time listening and reading, and only 10% speaking, slowly move that percentage towards the 50/50 mark. You have the daily fluency practice and all the spoken drills from this book to do this. Use the self-discipline practice from the previous chapter to force yourself to do the fluency practice, every day, no matter what.

The number one priority for most English learners should be to make their speaking skills as strong as their comprehension skills.

The best fruits are always at the top of the tree. To get the best fruits, you must climb the tree. Beyond that initial pain and discomfort lie the best rewards.

The most successful English learners are the ones that focus more on their English output. It's tempting to take the easy route and only focus on input. Just like a fish that takes the easy route by following the current and only going in the direction of the river flow. The most successful fish fight the flow of the river and don't take the easy route.

Why is that?

Because only dead fish go with the flow.

PRACTICE

HOW TO INCREASE YOUR PERCEIVED LEVEL OF ENGLISH

"Your English output must be equal to or greater than your English input."

The practice exercises I have shown you up to now have been drills designed to master individual aspects of English like speaking, listening, vocabulary and grammar. In Part 4, the final part of the book, the practice exercises are designed to make you an independent learner. They will teach you how to take control of your learning.

The drills I have shown you need to be done on a daily basis. The ones I will show you in Part 4 don't. Instead, I will show you practical learning exercises that will help you make continuous progress on your journey to mastering English on your own.

Let's look at the first: how to improve your perceived level of English.

Each English learner has three levels, not one, as everyone else will tell you.

You have your *academic level* of English, which is the level you get when you take an exam or finish a course. It's the level you put on your CV. This is what everybody thinks their only level is.

Then you have your *self-perceived level* of English, which is how you feel about your own level. It's related to how comfortable you are with your knowledge and use of English.

And then there is your *perceived level* of English. This is what others think about your knowledge and use of English.

Day 25

Your academic level mostly tells you how good you are at writing the correct answer on a piece of paper.

Your self-perceived and perceived levels of English tell you how well you can communicate in English.

> **LANGUAGE ISN'T WRITING CORRECT ANSWERS ON PAPER. LANGUAGE IS COMMUNICATION.**

Each of these levels can be drastically different from one another. For example, you can have a great academic level of English, but if you don't feel comfortable communicating and others have problems communicating with you, that level means nothing.

By far the most important levels are your self-perceived level and perceived level of English.

These two levels of English are directly proportional to your English output. The more output you have, the better you feel and the better others think of your English.

The more you speak and produce English, the more confident you will feel about your English.

Your self-perceived level and your perceived level are directly linked to each other. If you feel confident and comfortable using English, people recognise that and will think more positively of your English. Likewise, when others have a positive opinion of your use of English, this makes you feel more confident about your English.

The best way to increase your self-perceived level of English is by improving your confidence and control of English. The only way to do this is by speaking every day. The improvement in fluency and confidence is almost immediate.

There are three elements to improving your perceived level of English, which in turn will improve your self-perceived level.

1. Confidence
2. Few mistakes
3. Advanced vocabulary

1. Confidence

Confidence is by far the biggest factor in determining your perceived level of English, much more than mistakes. My friend Jorge gave a speech at my wedding in very broken English. It was full of mistakes, incorrect words and he didn't use grammar at all. However, everybody thought his English was excellent.

This is because he has a lot of self-confidence. He didn't care that he was making mistakes and he was engaged with the audience.

Humans respond more to how a person communicates and the impression that they give. They respond less to the words that the person says.

How can you become more confident?

By speaking. Speak every day and you will gain confidence very quickly. By improving your fluency, you gain control of your English. When you feel that you control your use of English, your confidence grows.

2. Few mistakes

Making fewer mistakes is a huge part of what this book is about. We covered this in detail in Part 2.

You should already have a very good idea of how to do this and you should be practising this on a daily basis.

Identify your mistakes and work to remove them. Find questions and doubts related to your use of English, then learn and practise them until you can use them correctly. Find language that you want to say but you don't know how. Identify your own weaknesses and work to improve them. And of course, if you are having a conversation with a person, ask them your questions and doubts as you speak.

The fewer mistakes you make, the better your English will be and the better you will feel about yourself.

3. **Advanced vocabulary**

When I say advanced vocabulary, what I mean is vocabulary that native speakers use. I don't mean difficult and complicated words. Many English learners make the mistake of thinking that advanced means complicated. Advanced English means you are able to express more with fewer words. Advanced vocabulary is everyday vocabulary that all native speakers use. You should use it too.

Your priority when learning vocabulary should be first to learn relevant vocabulary. Those words and phrases that you want to say but you don't know how.

On top of that, you should build your range of vocabulary by learning these four types of advanced vocabulary to sound more and more like a native speaker.

What vocabulary is this?

a. **Question tags.** You know the importance of question tags already and you know how to practise them.

b. **Adverbs.** English speakers love adverbs and they sound great. Sentence adverbs are the easiest to use. Simply begin the sentence with the adverb, followed by a comma. *Interestingly, Basically, Fortunately, Personally, Surprisingly,* are all examples of sentence adverbs. Other adverbs that have a powerful effect are adverbs that we use as single-word answers: *Indeed. Likewise. Absolutely. Totally.*

c. **Interjections.** We covered this on Day 7. These short phrases will really make you sound more like a native speaker. The best way to learn them is by watching films and series and listening carefully for them.

d. **Phrasal verbs.** Love them or hate them, there's no avoiding phrasal verbs. Native speakers love to use them so you must learn to love them too. Similar to grammar, the key to understanding them is situation and context, not the individual words that make up the phrasal verb.

Improving confidence, making fewer mistakes and learning advanced vocabulary should be at the forefront of your learning. When you make continuous progress in these areas, you feel fluent and comfortable speaking English.

Don't obsess over your academic level. Instead, aim to improve how you *feel* when you use English.

When you do that, you notice that you start to make more progress than ever.

Day 25

REVIEW

- *What does your own input/output graph look like?*
- *How much confidence do you have when you speak English?*
- *What can you do to help yourself feel more confident?*
- *How much better are you at identifying your own mistakes?*
- *Which of the four examples of advanced vocabulary do you least use?*
- *How can you improve them?*

Plan

Practise

Review

Reward

Do you want more practice? You can find an additional activity to practise the strategies from today's chapter in the free workbook. Visit www.how-to-english.com/workbook

DAY 26

HOW TO PLAN AND REACH YOUR GOALS

"How do you eat an elephant? One bite at a time." - **Proverb**

I want you to think for a moment about whatever goals you may have in your life right now.

What would you like to achieve this week? What about over the next six months? The next five years? What about a life goal?

And here's the most important question: how will you achieve those goals?

We all have goals. We all need goals.

Sometimes our goals seem impossible to reach, and we end up never achieving them. Often, though, it's not the goal that is difficult, but rather the path we take to get closer to the goal.

The destination isn't the problem. The journey to the destination is where the problems lie. It's easy to get lost, take the wrong path, lose energy and motivation, or never even plan your journey. If you don't plan your journey, you will never reach your destination.

> **THE JOURNEY TO YOUR GOAL IS MORE IMPORTANT THAN THE GOAL ITSELF.**

Today, I want to show you a technique I use to help people to create a goal. The best thing about this technique, however, is that it shows you exactly what you need to do to reach your goal.

It's an activity to help you think about what you want to improve and, more importantly, what you will do to achieve it. This is important because you can have a goal, but if you don't know exactly what you need to do to reach that goal, it's a waste of time.

For example, the vast majority of English learners do not plan their goals in English. They don't know what they want to improve in English. And of course, because they don't have any goals in English, they have no idea how they will achieve them.

Most English learners simply say, "I want to improve my English." That goal is far too general. As a result, their contact with English is very general, has no purpose, and they do activities in English at random.

It's hard to make progress this way.

When you start to set goals in your English learning and plan a way to achieve them, you start making more progress than you have ever made in your life.

This technique is perfect for English learners, but you can also use it for anything at all. I use it myself to plan my own goals and help me figure out a course of action.

I call this technique the **DNA-Plan**.

Sounds simple, doesn't it?

It is.

Just as your DNA is the smallest part of what constitutes you as a person, your DNA-Plan breaks down your goal into its smallest parts and tells you exactly what you want, what you need to do to achieve it and how you will reach it.

All you need to do is complete a series of statements, and the end result is a clear goal, a clear course of action and guaranteed success.

Day 26

We all have goals, some big and some small.

A huge problem with goal setting is that the bigger the goal, the less likely we are to start working towards it. The goals that we most want to achieve in life are often the ones that we never end up achieving.

WHY DOES THIS HAPPEN?

Well, there are a few reasons. One of them is what I call the big, scary elephant effect.

When you think about your biggest goal, it's often the fact that it seems so big (and therefore unrealistic) that we always try to avoid it. We continuously postpone it, saying we will start it later.

But as always, later becomes tomorrow.

And tomorrow becomes never.

The other reason is that people are not very good at creating milestones, something I explained on Day 16. Many people have a goal but have no idea how they will get there. They have no course of action.

Let me explain.

I call it the big, scary elephant effect in reference to the common proverb related to achieving goals:

> *"How do you eat an elephant?*
> *– One bite at a time"*

When you think about eating a whole elephant, metaphorically speaking, it can be quite intimidating and easy to put off.

When all you have to think about is taking one bite, then another bite later, it removes the big and scary thought of the bigger goal. If you take enough bites, eventually you eat the whole elephant.

People get stuck on what they want to achieve, their desire, but they don't have anything that they can act on.

It is only a desire, and a desire is nothing until it becomes action.

> **ONLY ACTION MATTERS.**

Take, for example, the classic goal of "I want to improve my English".

It's not really a goal.

First of all, it's much too general. How much English? Secondly, there is no clearly defined route, or a point at which they achieve this goal. And thirdly, there is nothing actionable. There is nothing the person can DO right now.

It's no surprise that it's one of the most common desires out there, and one that causes huge amounts of frustration.

They are stuck with their desire, their elephant. You need to take the desire of consuming a whole elephant and turn it into individual, actionable parts.

As I said, the person can't just improve their English today. But, the person can do something today that will help them to achieve that desire. And this is where you can use my DNA-Plan to break down a big goal into smaller, bite-size pieces.

The DNA-Plan takes this big, scary elephant (the person's desire), and breaks it down into small actions that you can take today.

The big, scary elephant will demotivate you. With this technique, you never have to think about your end goal or desire. You only have to think about and do one task at a time.

The natural result of reaching these small milestones every day will be that you achieve whatever goal you set.

It's simple, you can use it for anything, and it works.

Let me show you.

Here's what each letter in the DNA-Plan stands for:

D - This is your **Desire**, or the goal that you want to achieve.

N - This stands for **Need**, or what is fundamentally necessary in order for you to achieve your goal.

A - **Action**. This is where you think of those small, individual actions that you can take that are in alliance with your **Need**, and that move towards your **Desire**.

Plan - You have your actions or milestones, but you now need to decide exactly when you are going to do each of them. You put them into your practice plan for the week and schedule exactly what you will do and when.

Here's an example:

Desire: I want to improve my listening skills.

Starting with a desire gets you thinking about what you want to achieve.

Need: To do this, I need to practise listening in English every day.

The need is what is fundamentally necessary in order for the desire to become a reality. The desire can never be a reality without this essential part. However, it's still a little too general.

Action: To do this, I can do dictations, listen to the radio, watch films or series, listen to an audiobook, ...

This is where you get creative. You think of individual actions, small bites of the elephant, that you can take today, right now. Think of as many as you can. The focus is on small, daily, easy-to-achieve actions.

Plan: I'm going to listen to the radio every day when I wake up. I'm going to do an activity to listen for specific information on my way to work. I'm going to do dictations on Mondays, Wednesdays and Fridays during the first ten minutes of my lunch break. I'm going to listen to 30 minutes of an audiobook while I prepare dinner. I'm going to watch a film in English on Saturday evenings.

Finally, you plan when, where and how you will do each. Write them in your practice plan for the week. As you schedule them, you should be even more specific and include links to the dictations that you will do, the radio station you will listen to, the number of chapters of the audiobook, and so on. Don't leave anything out.

By scheduling these actions, you commit yourself to the task. You also realise that it's actually really easy to do these little tasks.

Forget the elephant. Plan the bites, then take one bite at a time.

The difficult part of achieving a goal is never the end goal itself. It's creating the goal, taking the first steps and sticking with it that's difficult.

This technique removes all those obstacles so all you have to think about is taking one "bite", then another, then another.

Do this exercise once a week to plan your next week, and you never need to worry about achieving your goal or being motivated. Just plan the route towards your goal, then take small steps towards it every day.

Do this with all of your goals. Both on a weekly basis to help you plan the week and on a monthly basis for longer-term goals. It gives you full control over your future and you will never need to think about what you need to do. You do the DNA-Plan once, then all you need to do is reach those milestones that you wrote down in your plan.

If you just take small bites, the natural result is that you will achieve whatever you want.

Now go eat that elephant.

Day 26

PRACTICE

HOW TO COMPLETE YOUR FIRST DNA-PLAN

"If you don't take control of your future, later becomes tomorrow, and tomorrow becomes never."

Your practice exercise for today will be to complete your first DNA-Plan to create a plan for next week, after you finish this book.

At the moment, you have me to guide you through the process of taking control of your English. But next week, you will be on your own, and you will need to be completely independent as an English learner.

Your practice plan should always include the daily fluency practice, reading fiction, some general listening practice and dictations. On top of this, you should also include a short-term goal that includes activities and practice exercises that move you towards your weekly goal.

The purpose of the DNA-Plan is to improve in a specific area of English. One specific improvement per week. Your DNA-Plan will help you decide what you want to achieve and how you will do it.

WHAT SHOULD YOU HAVE AS YOUR GOAL?

An area of weakness. Identify a weakness in your English and use that as your goal.

So let's do it. Let's plan next week. Complete the following sentences with whatever you want:

Desire: I want to…

Need: To do this, I need to…

Action: To do this, I can…

Plan: I'm going to do [what] [when] and [what] [when]…

Now take your practice plan for next week and schedule each action. Say exactly what you will do and when you will do it, including links and the length of time for each action.

I also recommend creating two plans. One for your English learning and another for some personal goal that you would like to achieve. The beauty of the DNA-Plan is that you can use it for anything.

I guarantee that if you do it, you will achieve the goal that you set.

Leonardo da Vinci once said that simplicity is the ultimate sophistication. The DNA-Plan is about as simple and sophisticated as you can get.

REVIEW

- *What goal did you set recently that you failed to achieve?*
- *Why did you fail to achieve it?*
- *How can you avoid making the same mistake again?*
- *What English goal would you like to achieve next week?*
- *What personal goal would you like to achieve in the next month?*
- *What's your biggest desire in English?*

Plan

Practise

Review

Reward

DAY 27

HOW TO CREATE AND COMPLETE YOUR OWN INTENSIVE COURSE

*"One inch wide and one mile deep is better than
one mile wide and one inch deep."*

A Jack of all trades, master of none. It can often be very useful to be this kind of person. You have many skills, but you aren't an expert in any of them.

With a language, though, it can cause a few problems if you learn in this way.

One of the most common English learning mistakes that people make is that they don't learn grammar and vocabulary to the point at which they can use it comfortably and confidently.

They only scratch the surface of the learning process.

The result of not learning elements of English perfectly is that you end up with a head full of unconsolidated language. Language that you may understand, but you don't feel that you can use confidently. And a head full of unconsolidated language is one of the most frustrating feelings an English learner can have.

They have a lot of knowledge in their head, but they don't know how to use it.

WHAT'S BETTER, TO LEARN LOTS OF LANGUAGE BADLY OR TO LEARN A LITTLE VERY WELL?

I'll let you decide.

What is certain is that if you are going to learn something with the intention of using it, it's better to learn it well than it is to learn it badly. And if you're learning English, it's probably because you need to use it.

To learn something in depth, you first need to get a very good understanding of it. The best way to do this is to get the information from multiple sources. Each source will give you their version of what is true. When multiple sources of information teach you the same topic, you get a much better understanding of it. The key is not to depend 100% on one source of information.

And you know this already. Depending on your objective, you will choose to learn something superficially or in depth.

If you only want to understand it, maybe you will only need one explanation. But if you want to use it, you will need more than one explanation and you will need to practise it too.

Take the expression that I used in the first sentence of this chapter as an example: a Jack of all trades, master of none. Maybe you hadn't seen this expression before. If you only want to understand it, you can look it up in a dictionary, see what it means so you can understand the sentence, and the work is done. But if you like the expression and you decide that you want to use it in the future, you will need to do a little more. You will need to find out in what situations you can use this expression, in what situations you can't and how to actually use it in a sentence.

Makes sense, right?

If people know this already, why do they make the mistake of only learning elements of English superficially?

Day 27

Because people think that if they understand something in English, they know it. But that's not exactly true.

If you can't use what you understand, you don't really know it.

> **KNOWING IS NOTHING,
> USING WHAT YOU KNOW IS EVERYTHING.**

If you really know something, you understand it *and* you can use it.

Everything that you learn in English you should learn with this in mind. You want to avoid having unconsolidated knowledge in your head at all cost. It's a waste of energy and it doesn't help you make progress. If anything, it slows you down.

Learn it until you can use it comfortably and confidently.

How can you do this on your own?

By creating your own intensive course.

The world we live in is an incredible place right now. We are all connected. You have all the knowledge of the world literally at your fingertips. You can learn anything you want at will.

And that includes English.

Everything you will ever need to master English on your own you can find either in your head or online.

Let me show you how you can create and complete your own intensive course.

During your fluency practice, you will identify problems that you have with particular aspects of English. Imagine you are speaking about next week and you want to say a sentence, but you don't know whether to use *will* or *going to* in your sentence. You realise that there is something about these two structures that you don't completely understand.

Fantastic!

That means you have identified something relevant to learn. The most important thing is to identify relevant language. You don't want to waste energy and time learning something that you will never use.

Now you have identified something to learn, you need to build an intensive course around it.

All you need to do to get a full understanding of this grammar point is watch one video per day and read one online lesson per day. There are thousands and thousands of English teachers that provide free video and written lessons online.

What you first need are explanations of this grammar point so you can understand it. To get this, do an online search for the grammar point + *explanation*: *"will going to explanation"*. Hundreds or thousands of videos and online lessons will come up in the results. Don't do thousands, only the first five.

Put the first five videos in your practice plan for the week plus the first five online written lessons that appear in the results. Do one of each every day for five days. On the sixth day, to check that you understood those explanations, do a search for the grammar point + *practice exercises*: *"will going to practice exercises"*.

Do the first five.

After those six days, you will have a complete understanding of *will* and *going to*.

That's the input part covered. Now for the most important part: output.

Now you need to use the language you have just learned.

Use it as part of your fluency practice and in drills for a whole week. Have it as your focus for the week. Play with the language and manipulate it. This is the only way to consolidate the language in your head.

Day 27

If you only watch one video or read one online lesson, you will not completely understand it. If you don't do the output part of the practice, you will not be able to use it.

> **YOU NEED QUALITY INPUT AND QUALITY OUTPUT.**

The following week, identify a new weakness in your grammar and repeat the process. Use the **DNA-Plan** to identify exactly what you want to learn, how you will learn it, and how you will practise it. Then add it to your practice plan.

Slowly but surely, you will cover all of your weaknesses in English and you will get perfect grammar.

It's a simple process, and it guarantees that everything that you learn, you learn completely. You will be able to use the language comfortably and confidently. By learning each grammar point completely and consolidating it with drills, you get rid of mistakes and give yourself a strong foundation of grammar.

If you're going to build a house, it's better to have strong foundations.

PRACTICE

HOW TO USE ONLINE DICTIONARIES AND SOCIAL MEDIA

"Feed the habit and savour the rewards."

Technology is great. It enables us to be connected at all times. That can sometimes be good and sometimes be bad.

For the purpose of English learning, it's definitely a good thing, if you use it correctly. If you want to know something - anything - you can find the answer in a few seconds on your mobile.

I've already explained how you can master any grammar point by searching for videos and lessons, doing practice exercises online and practising it.

Now I'll show you how you can use online dictionaries and social media to boost learning.

VOCABULARY

With vocabulary, you should definitely follow a system to make sure that when you learn a new word or phrase, you learn it until you are able to use it without mistakes.

A typical mistake that English learners make is that when they see a word for the first time, they quickly look it up in a bilingual dictionary for a translation and think that all the work is done.

That will help you understand the word, but you probably won't be able to use it in the future if you *only* do that. You need to do a little more.

Looking up a new word in a bilingual dictionary is essential, but it's only the first step in the process of being able to use the word.

Day 27

When you have a translation of the word, you should then put the word into an English dictionary. You do this to get the full definition with example sentences. This is important as there may be small differences in definition or use between the word in English and the word in your own language.

Next, look up the word in a dictionary that shows the word in context, like Linguee. The great thing about this type of dictionary is that it shows the word in multiple sentences so you can understand the situation and context that it is used in. This is important as it tells you how to use the word or phrase.

Last of all, look up the word in a thesaurus. A thesaurus is a dictionary that groups words together according to their definition. It gives you synonyms of the word you look up. This helps you broaden your range of vocabulary.

All the steps in this simple and quick process help you get a better understanding of the word as well as how to use it. But there's an added bonus to following a system like this: it helps you remember the word you are trying to learn. Each dictionary helps you memorise the word by seeing it in multiple contexts and reading multiple definitions.

The final step is to then practise and use the word in drills to solidify your understanding of its meaning and use.

Follow these steps and you will easily remember every new word you learn, as well as how and when to use it.

SOCIAL MEDIA

Whichever social networking service you use, you can guarantee that there will be hundreds or thousands of English teachers providing free content on a daily basis.

All you need to do is search online for the most popular hashtags that English teachers use to tag their content, then find and follow the ones that you like most.

The social networking service that you use will then send you notifications every time one of the English teachers that you follow uploads something new. This is fantastic because you receive free mini-lessons directly to your mobile.

The bad thing about using social media for learning English is that you obviously have no control over the lessons that you receive. You will receive whatever the teachers choose to post at that time.

You certainly cannot depend on social media teachers to provide all your learning needs. Far from it. The same goes for apps. You cannot depend on apps to improve your English. Download a few, play around with them, but do not depend on them.

The best thing about social media for English learning is that it keeps the English part of your brain ready and alert all day. Every notification will remind you that you are learning English and will maintain your curiosity for learning. It will also provide you with an opportunity to find questions or doubts about English, which you can then go and find the answers to on your own.

Social media can be great to help maintain your curiosity, receive mini-lessons all day and learn new language, but don't depend on it for all your learning needs. Remember, the most powerful learning machine you have is sitting inside your head right now.

Depend on your own brain to learn and master English.

Day 27

REVIEW

- *What words, phrases and grammar do you understand but don't know how to use perfectly?*
- *What can you do to learn how to use them perfectly over the next week?*
- *How many dictionaries do you normally use when you look up a new word?*
- *Do you follow any social media English teachers?*

Plan

Practise

Review

Reward

DAY 28

HOW TO MAKE SHORT-TERM, MID-TERM AND LONG-TERM GOALS

*"When a river stops moving, the water goes bad.
The same thing happens with humans."*

My legs felt like jelly.

I was exhausted. Every step hurt. But finally, after forty-two kilometres, I could see the finish line. At that point, I wanted it to end as quickly as possible. As I crossed the finish line with my arms in the air, I wanted it to last forever.

I cried. Then I laughed. I felt on top of the world.

But then something strange happened.

After finishing my first marathon, I didn't run again for almost a month. I felt less motivated than ever to go out running. It was my passion, and I had just achieved one of my biggest goals ever.

"What has happened to me?", I thought.

When I went out running again, it was the last thing I wanted to do. I had to push myself out the door again and again for a week or so. Then I signed up for another race, and all the motivation came back.

As I explained on Day 16, the time when you often feel least motivated to continue is when you reach your goal.

It seems paradoxical, but it makes perfect sense.

> **HUMANS NEED TO BE MOVING. WE NEED TO BE MOVING TOWARDS SOMETHING.**

What exactly?

It doesn't matter, as long as you are moving towards it. The better the objective, the better for you. The brain, however, only wants to move towards an objective.

As you move towards your objective, you feel motivated. That is all motivation is. Motivation is not about reaching your objective. It's the feeling that you are moving closer to your objective.

There is a huge difference between the two.

What happens when you reach your goal is that you no longer have anything to move towards. If you aren't moving closer to an objective, you feel no motivation. This is exactly why many people on a diet start to put weight on again when they reach their target weight.

WITH THAT IN MIND, WHAT IS THE SECRET TO ALWAYS FEELING MOTIVATED?

Exactly. Always have an objective that you can move towards. So many English learners simply don't have goals or the goals that they set are far too general. The result is that they walk around with no aim, then they get lost and frustrated. Or worse, they do nothing.

Always have a goal to move towards.

WHAT'S BETTER THAN HAVING ONE GOAL?

Right. Having more than one goal. Multiple goals in multiple time frames, to be precise.

This is something I recommend to every English learner I speak to. Anybody who wants to improve their English in the most efficient and effective way and enjoy the process needs to have multiple goals in multiple time frames.

Day 28

Do you want to improve your English efficiently, effectively and enjoy the process?

Great. Then read on.

You need to have three goals: one short-term, one mid-term and one long-term.

Having three goals in different time frames allows you to regularly reach goals and work towards a bigger goal in the future.

Let me explain each of the goals.

1. **Short-term goal**

    Your short-term goal is a goal or set of goals that you complete every week. One day per week, you sit down and write out everything that you want to achieve during the following week.

    Sound familiar?

    That's right. It's your practice plan.

    Your practice plan is your set of goals for the coming week. You decide what activities you will do. You choose particular activities based on your weaknesses, language that you want to improve and skills that you would like to improve. You create the plan for the week using the **DNA-Plan.**

    Your goal is to complete these tasks and activities.

    You should be extremely proud of yourself every time you achieve this weekly goal.

    Congratulate yourself every time you complete one of the activities in your practice plan, and even more so when you finish the weekly plan. It's a massive achievement. And it's something that you can achieve every single week.

    Your short-term goal is your practice plan.

2. **Mid-term goal**

    Your mid-term goal is a challenge.

    It's important to make the process of learning English interesting and challenging.

    Having a challenge helps you perform the best you can.

    Your mid-term goal is a challenge that you work towards over the course of a month or two. It must be something that requires some effort and discomfort, but something that you can achieve and want to achieve.

    Example challenges could be to volunteer to give a presentation at work in English, call a stranger in an English-speaking country every day for a month, meet and introduce yourself to ten native speakers in a month, read a whole book in English with a tight deadline, learn 150 new words in a month, listen to the *War and Peace* audiobook (over 60 hours long) in two months, and so on.

    You get the idea.

    Your mid-term goal or challenge should be something that you would prefer to avoid. That way you can practise and improve self-discipline too. It should be a little scary and intimidating, but also something that you can absolutely achieve with consistent effort. It is more difficult than your short-term goal, but it makes the journey interesting, and the reward and satisfaction you get from completing it is far greater.

    Your time frame for your mid-term goal should be one to two months. When you are halfway through, start thinking about the next one.

    Humans perform best when we have a little adversity. Not too much adversity, but some. Humans perform worst when everything is easy. Your mid-term goal or challenge will give you the perfect amount of adversity to make you perform the best you can.

3. **Long-term goal**

    If your short-term goals are actions and your mid-term goal is a challenge, your long-term goal should be a skill that you can't do now but

Day 28

you would like to be able to do in six months to a year.

Think of something that you currently cannot do in English. There may be many things that you cannot do. Choose the one which most frustrates you.

That should be your long-term goal.

Many people make the mistake of creating a long-term goal which is far too general. The classic example is, "I want to improve my English."

Instead, complete the sentence, "I want to be able to…" to help you get some ideas.

"I want to be able to give a presentation in English at work comfortably and confidently", "I want to be able to watch films and series without subtitles", or "I want to be able to use all the tenses in English perfectly" are just a few good examples.

Each long-term goal will influence how you practise as you work towards it. In the first example above, the person should focus on fluency and building their confidence. In the second, they should concentrate on listening. In the third, they should work on perfecting each tense, one by one over the course of a year.

When you sit down to plan your next week (your short-term goal), take a moment to set a mid-term and long-term goal too, and start working towards them.

Without goals, you never move. Not moving is the worst thing you can do. When a river stops moving, the water goes bad. That's exactly what happens when humans stop moving.

Always have something to work on and move towards. As long as you keep moving, you will achieve all your goals and feel great along the way.

PRACTICE

HOW TO MODIFY OR CHANGE YOUR ENGLISH PRACTICE

"Sometimes you don't need to change what you do, but rather when and where you do it."

When I first started writing, I hated it.

Every time I had to write, I would sit down, groan and complain, then write for an hour or two. I was so happy when it finished. I wanted to do anything except write.

It was the least enjoyable obligation that I had.

I thought that over time I would start to enjoy writing, but I didn't. I continued to dislike writing for months. Eventually, I accepted that it was just something that I didn't like, but a task that I had to do, whether I liked it or not.

But early one morning, one of my children woke me up to go to the bathroom at 5 o'clock in the morning. I tried to go back to sleep again, but it was no good. I was awake. I thought that if I couldn't sleep, I could at least spend the time wisely. So I decided to do some writing. I sat down at the computer, wrote until 7 o'clock and absolutely loved it.

I wrote more in those two hours than in the entire previous week. Writing felt easy and even enjoyable. I was so productive I couldn't believe it.

Just like that, I suddenly loved writing.

THAT FIRST DAY WAS ONE OF MY BEST DAYS OF WORK EVER.

Day 28

From then on, I started waking up at 5.30am every morning to write. I felt stupid that I hadn't thought of doing it before. It seemed so obvious. Until then, I had been writing in the evening in the living room, tired and my head full of the stresses of the day. In the morning, I felt fresh, alert, motivated and incredibly productive.

The problem wasn't *what* I was doing, but rather *when* I was doing it. It was such a simple solution to a long-term problem.

I didn't hate writing; I hated writing in the evening.

A few months later, however, I started to notice that writing was becoming difficult again. I still enjoyed it, but I wasn't as productive as before. I thought about this problem and came to the conclusion that I was doing it at the right *time*, but maybe I wasn't doing it in the right *place*.

The next day, instead of sitting down in the living room to write, I decided to go to the kitchen. My productivity immediately improved again.

This time, the problem wasn't *what* I was doing, but rather *where* I was doing it.

Again, it seemed so obvious. I felt stupid that I hadn't thought of it before. Of course, something only seems obvious after you change it for something better.

That's hindsight for you...

It wasn't the activity that was the problem, it was the environment. It wasn't what I was doing that was the problem, it was when and where I was doing it.

All I needed to do was change when and where I wrote, and the problems instantly disappeared.

I'm not saying you should wake up at 5.30am every day and practise

English in your kitchen. All I'm saying is that your environment has a massive effect on you and how you feel. It sometimes affects you more than the activity itself.

If there is an activity in English that you don't enjoy or that feels difficult, maybe it's not the activity that is the problem. It might be that it's when or where you are doing it.

Check, modify or change your environment to make sure it gives you the best results possible. You want the time you spend in contact with English to be as productive, effective and enjoyable as possible. To do that, check your environment, and modify it or change it if it doesn't give you those results.

And of course you want your English time to be as productive and enjoyable as possible. Otherwise, you just waste your time and hate the process. Who wants that?

Take a moment to review your practice plan from last week. Have a look at when and where you did each activity and think about how you felt during and after the activity. Did you feel productive during the activity? Did you feel motivated and happy after?

Experiment with different locations and times and see how you feel as a result.

The crazy thing is that you can never predict what will work. It either works or it doesn't. Sometimes you don't even know why it works, it just does.

EXPERIMENT

I had no idea that 5.30am was the best time for me to write. I had no idea the kitchen would be better for writing than the living room.

For whatever reason, I'm more productive in the kitchen at 5.30am.

Go figure.

Day 28

Find your perfect time and place to have contact with English. You will be more productive and you will enjoy it more.

Everything will feel easier.

REVIEW

- *What do you have in mind for your first challenge?*
- *What would you like to be able to do in one year that you can't do now?*
- *When and where do you most enjoy practising English?*
- *When and where do you least enjoy it?*

Plan

Practise

Review

Reward

DAY 29

HOW TO CONTROL WHAT YOU LEARN AND HOW YOU LEARN

*"When you learn how to learn,
you never need to worry about what you learn."*

There are two big, ugly truths in the English teaching world that nobody likes to talk about.

The first is the problem of what you learn. I explained earlier in the book that the big problem of what you learn in a classroom is that as you improve in level, the teaching material becomes less and less relevant. This is because as you increase in level, your own language needs start to become more and more personal.

At the beginner levels, every teacher knows exactly what every learner should learn. All the material is relevant to each and every student at these levels, because the needs of each and every student at these levels are exactly the same for everybody.

When you start to improve in level, you start to have your own personal needs. You will make grammar mistakes that only you make. You will have your own vocabulary needs, which are the words and phrases that you need in order to feel that you express yourself as you would like to.

Each student has their own grammar problems and vocabulary needs that are exclusive to them.

It is at this point that the learner needs to start taking control of their own learning.

If they don't, they start to get frustrated. And they will continue to feel frustrated unless they do something about it.

This brings us to the second problem, which is how you learn. Most people have a huge misconception in their head. They think that in order to learn a language, they have to go to classes. But we've been learning foreign languages for tens of thousands of years without classes. It's only in the last few hundred years that we have had organised and structured foreign language classes.

> **THE BRAIN IS PERFECTLY ADAPTED TO LEARNING LANGUAGES. WE HAVE JUST FORGOTTEN HOW.**

Classes and teachers are not bad. They can and should be great learning environments. What is bad is depending on teachers and classes in order to learn and make progress.

If you depend on teachers and classes to learn, you will always need teachers and classes to learn.

Then you start a vicious circle of depending on classes to improve, but what you learn in class becomes less and less relevant. Then, when you stop attending classes, you start losing your level.

And the cycle of frustration continues.

That is not a solution.

HOW CAN YOU CONTROL WHAT YOU LEARN AND HOW YOU LEARN?

Let me show you.

And let me tell you that what I'm about to explain is everything you will ever need to know about what to learn and how to learn.

Let's take a look at the following diagram, which covers everything you need to know about how to learn English.

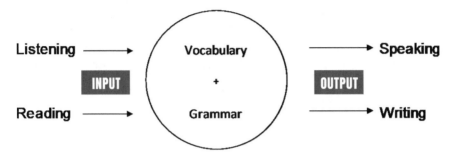

Language in its cold, lifeless form is vocabulary and grammar.

Just like a house, which in its basic form is made up of bricks and mortar.

However, humans are not cold and lifeless, and we interact with languages. We interact with the language using the four skills. Those skills are listening, reading, speaking and writing.

We can interact with the language passively. This is when the language comes to us and we absorb and process it. We can interact with the language passively by listening and by reading. We use the senses of the ears and eyes to do this. This is what I call *input*.

But of course, we can also interact with the language actively, by producing it. We can interact with the language actively by speaking (fluency and pronunciation are part of this) and by writing. We use our mouth and hands to do this. This is what I call *output*.

The combination of these is everything you need to know about a language. You have the parts of the language (grammar and vocabulary) and how we interact with the language (the skills).

All you need to do is learn some and improve others.

You *learn* grammar and vocabulary and *improve* the four skills.

HOW CAN YOU DO THIS IN THE BEST WAY POSSIBLE?

Let's look at the learning part first. Grammar and vocabulary are the only two aspects of English that you actually need to *learn*. Everything else you need to *improve*. You need to learn grammar, and you need to learn vocabulary. If you are B1 or above, you don't actually need to learn much more grammar. You need to learn to make fewer mistakes. You've been learning grammar all your life.

It's a small but important difference.

It's now time to identify and remove your mistakes. If you make fewer mistakes, your grammar improves. If you don't make any mistakes, your grammar is perfect. Learn to make fewer mistakes.

If you only need to learn grammar and vocabulary, what grammar and vocabulary should you learn? Or, how can you make everything you learn 100% relevant?

There are only two things you need to learn to guarantee that everything you learn is relevant to you:

1. Corrections of the mistakes that you make
2. Things that you want to say, but you don't know how

If you only learn these two things, everything you learn will be relevant to you. If you learn the corrections of the mistakes you make, your grammar improves. If you learn words and phrases that you want to say, but you don't know how, you will learn relevant vocabulary.

Prioritise learning these two over everything else.

Day 29

WHAT ABOUT THE SKILLS?

You don't learn the skills you use to interact with English, you improve them.

Which ones should you improve?

First, you create your own input/output graph, which shows you how competent you feel with each of the skills. To do this, decide on a scale of one to ten, how you feel with regard to each skill, according to your level. By doing this, you will see where you need to spend most of your time and effort.

Here's an example of a student who has just completed their first input/output graph.

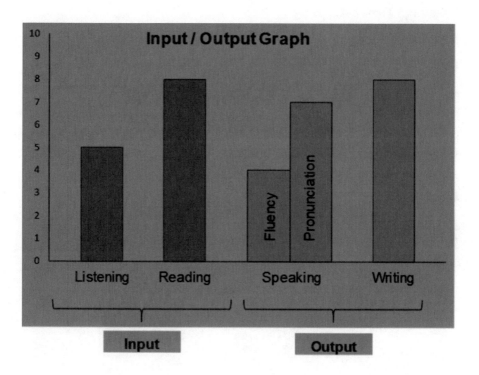

You can see that they have the most input problems with listening, and they feel quite comfortable reading. In the output part, they have the most difficulties speaking, particularly with fluency. They feel relatively comfortable writing.

The results from the graph will tell you how you should spend most of your contact time with English and how much you need to improve each skill.

From this graph, we can see that this English learner should spend most of their contact with English speaking and listening. That will tell the learner how to organise their practice plan for the following week.

You should always practise whatever your biggest problem is. Is your biggest problem speaking? Then speak more. Is your biggest problem listening? Then listen more.

Learn to make fewer mistakes and learn more relevant vocabulary. Improve the skills you use to interact with English.

WHAT IS THE BEST THING THAT YOU CAN LEARN IN ENGLISH?

Corrections of your mistakes, and words and phrases that you want to say, but you don't know how.

HOW SHOULD YOU LEARN IN ENGLISH?

By practising the skills which you have most difficulties with.

That is how you solve the biggest problem in the English teaching world. And it's your secret weapon to master English.

Day 29

PRACTICE

HOW TO REVIEW AND CHECK YOUR OWN PROGRESS

*"If I give up now, I'll be back where I started.
When I started, I wanted to be where I am now."*

You have created your own goals. You have short-term, mid-term and long-term goals.

You have started your journey towards taking control of your own English progress. On your journey, it's important to stop and take a look around to see if you are still going in the right direction.

Yesterday, you learned how to check and review both your English practice and your environment. Today, it's time to check your own progress so you can identify exactly what you are doing well and what needs to change.

That way you can be sure that you are always on the path which best leads you to your destination.

> **CHECK YOUR PROGRESS, THEN MODIFY OR CHANGE YOUR PROCESS.**

At the end of every day, every week and every month, take a moment to reflect on your progress. It only takes a minute. Check the results that you are getting, modify where necessary and change what doesn't work for something else.

Check, then modify or change.

Do more of what works and less of what doesn't work. That will always keep you on the right track.

When you check your progress, you look into the past. You can only measure progress by looking into the past. Your aim today is to be a little bit better in English than you were yesterday. If you do this continuously, over time you make massive progress.

When you look into the past and see what went well and what didn't go so well, it tells you how you should continue into the future. Creating your practice plan becomes extremely easy.

Your practice plan is the map you use to get to your destination.

Without a map, you can never reach your destination.

Today I will give you some questions that you can use to check your own progress. The answers to these questions will tell you how to plan your future, both short-term and long-term. At the end of each day, ask and answer the questions about **today** and **tomorrow**. At the end of each week, ask and answer the questions about **last week** and **next week**. Then do the same for **last month** and **next month**.

Answer these questions slowly and out loud. Think about your answers carefully and be honest with yourself.

And of course, add your own questions that you feel are specific to you.

Last month
- *How much progress have I made in the last month?*
- *What have I made the most progress in?*
- *What can I do now that I couldn't do one month ago?*
- *How have I improved my weaknesses in the last month?*
- *What progress have I made towards reaching my mid-term and long-term goals?*
- *What can I be proud of having achieved over the last month?*

Day 29

Last week

- *How did last week go?*
- *What was the best thing about last week?*
- *What goals did I set and reach?*
- *Which goals did I set, but didn't reach?*
- *Why didn't I reach them?*
- *What should I do next time to make sure I reach them?*
- *Can I change any practice exercises to make them more productive?*
- *Can I change my environment in some way to make it more productive?*
- *What can I be proud of having achieved over the last week?*

Today

- *What was the best thing about today?*
- *Why was it so good?*
- *What difficulties did I have?*
- *Did I overcome those difficulties? Why/why not?*
- *What can I be proud of today?*

Tomorrow

- *What is my main focus tomorrow?*
- *How can I make sure I achieve it?*
- *How can I make tomorrow better than today?*
- *What potential obstacles are there tomorrow?*
- *How can I overcome them?*
- *What can I do tomorrow that will make me proud of myself?*

Next week

- *What is my main focus for next week?*
- *What new language do I need to practise more next week?*
- *How can next week be better than this week?*
- *Can I modify or change any activities or the environment in some way?*
- *Are there any obstacles that I need to plan for next week?*
- *What can I do next week that will make me proud of myself?*

Next month

- *What skill do I want to improve most next month?*
- *How can I move closer to my mid-term and long-term goals?*
- *What can I do to maintain the habit?*
- *Will there be any obstacles next month?*
- *How can I overcome them?*
- *What can I do that will make me proud of myself?*

Day 29

REVIEW

*"The words that you use when you talk to yourself
are the words that have the most profound effect on your life."*

Your review questions for today are the above progress check questions.

Plan

Practise

Review

Reward

DAY 30

MOTIVATION, SELF-DISCIPLINE AND HABITS (PART 4)
HOW TO CREATE A HABIT

*"Most of your efforts should go into practising
keeping the habit of learning English,
not practising English."*

What's the difference between an architect and a builder?

An architect designs the house and gives the instructions to the builder. The builder follows the instructions.

In traditional teaching, the teacher is the architect and the student is the builder.

BUT YOU ARE DIFFERENT.

Yes, you're building a language in your head. Slowly but surely, you are putting all the pieces of English together to build the language. But you are not only a builder. You also decide what to learn and how to learn.

You are the builder *and* the architect. That is a powerful combination.

WHAT IS YOUR GOAL TODAY AS ARCHITECT AND BUILDER?

I will tell you what it isn't. Your goal is not to build the house. As the old saying goes, Rome wasn't built in a day. Your goal today is to lay a brick. Just one brick. But when you lay that brick, you need to lay it the best you can. It needs to fit perfectly with the brick next to it. It should be a strong and essential part of the whole house.

Because it is. A badly laid brick can bring the whole house to the ground.

All you need to do today is lay one brick the best you can. You are only going to do one thing today, but you are going to do it perfectly.

Tomorrow, lay another brick. Again, perfectly.

WHY DO YOU THINK THERE ARE THIRTY-ONE DAYS IN THIS BOOK?

Because I want you to do something every day. I want you to realise that doing something in English every day isn't as difficult as you thought. I want you to be consistent.

I want you to create a habit.

I want you to create the habit of laying one brick every day. I want you to continue laying bricks when you finish this book. To do that, you need to practise laying bricks for a month.

Consistency is the key.

If you can master consistency, you will master English.

Consistency is habit, and the brain loves habit. It doesn't matter if that habit is good or bad. It just needs to be a habit. The vast majority of all your actions in a typical day are habit.

WHY DOES THE BRAIN LIKE HABIT SO MUCH?

Because when the brain follows a habit, it doesn't need to think or make decisions to complete a task. It can run on autopilot and save energy.

Your brain only cares about saving energy. And thinking and making decisions uses a lot of energy.

This is why your practice plan is the most important aspect of all your

English learning. When you sit down and make all the learning decisions for a whole week, you don't need to make any other decisions about English learning for a whole week. You just look at your plan and do what it says.

Building a habit is essential if you want to reach your goals.

There's a misconception related to building a new habit. Many people think that after twenty-one days, a month or another period of time, the new habit becomes automatic. Then what happens is that they complete the period of time, become stressed because it isn't automatic, then give up.

It's not automatic after the "promised" period of time. It just requires less effort to keep the habit.

You will always need to work on keeping the habit. But keeping the habit will require less effort than when you started.

HOW CAN YOU MAKE IT EASY TO KEEP THE HABIT?

The first step is to plan everything. And I mean everything. Not just English practice, but also time off English. You have a holiday? Plan around it. Take a week or two off; don't feel bad. English should never feel like a prison. Plan your time off in advance and plan exactly when you will start again.

The second step is to make the new habit something that you can sustain. Your priority is not to practise English only today. Your priority is to practise English today in a way that will make you want to practise again tomorrow.

Your priority is today, tomorrow, the next day, next week and next month.

You can make English practice sustainable by making it easy to achieve. Here's how you can do that.

When people set a goal, they often focus on the minimum amount of work they need to do. The problem with that is that it can make reaching the goal seem a little stressful. It feels as if you are always moving uphill. The trick is to also set a maximum limit. If you set a maximum, it makes the task seem easier to complete.

Look at the following two goals for today:

1. I want to read at least 10 pages today.
2. I want to read at least 10 pages today, but no more than 15.

When you set a minimum and maximum amount of practice, it becomes easier to achieve the minimum.

WHY IS THAT?

Because the brain focuses more on the upper limit. You focus more on when you can rest and not what you must achieve.

It also gives you the flexibility to do more if you feel like it or have time.

When you start a new habit, give yourself only a maximum. This is exactly what I recommend with fluency practice: no more than five minutes at a time.

At first, start with a very low maximum. You want it to be so low that there is no excuse for not doing it. No more than five minutes of fluency practice, no more than one page of a book, no more than five minutes of listening, no more than one minute of dictation. As you get used to the new habit, you can increase the maximum.

When you only have a minimum, you only do the minimum, and it feels like an obligation. When you give yourself a maximum, it becomes easy to achieve the minimum.

Doing a lot of practice one day means nothing if you don't do it again the next day.

Day 30

WHAT MATTERS IS DOING IT AGAIN.

If you consistently do what you say you will do, you create a habit, and success is inevitable. Success in English has nothing to do with luck. Success is 100% dependent on your habits.

Take the decision to reach all of your learning goals, apply the basic principles, and you will succeed.

I guarantee it.

It's all about habit. You design a habit and then work to keep it.

And you can do that because you are the architect *and* the builder in your English learning.

PRACTICE

HOW TO EXPRESS YOURSELF PERFECTLY

*"Everybody can but not everybody will.
Be the person that can and will."*

Do you ever have the feeling that you always express yourself in the same way, using the same vocabulary?

Do you feel that the way you express yourself in English doesn't reflect who you really are?

It's annoying, isn't it?

Many English learners feel like this. And of course, they don't know what to do to stop feeling like this.

Expressing yourself clearly means choosing the right words for the right situation. But each person also has their own way of expressing themselves, and the words they use should reflect how they like to communicate.

Perfect expression means using the right words for the situation, and the right words for how you like to communicate.

Because there are many different ways to interpret a particular situation, you need a variety of ways to express the same idea. When you have a variety of different ways to express the same idea, you can choose the one which best reflects the situation you are in.

All you need to do is learn different ways to express the same idea.

This is slightly different from building a wide range of vocabulary. The focus here is to use the vocabulary that you already know to express the same idea in a variety of ways.

Take the typical example of commenting on nice weather. There are many different ways to express this, often with a question tag. Here are a few examples:

Lovely day, isn't it?

We're having great weather today, aren't we?

Marvellous weather, isn't it?

Beautiful day, don't you think?

The weather's nice today, isn't it?

Having more than one way to express an idea gives you more options to choose from. This makes you express yourself perfectly.

Take a sentence, any sentence, and think of as many different ways to express that idea as possible. You will probably be able to think of a couple very quickly. When you can't think of any more, try to think of others in your own language. Write them down then find a way to translate them into English.

Here's another example.

My laptop is slower than it was.

My laptop was faster before.

My laptop isn't as fast as it was.

My laptop wasn't as slow as it is now.

My laptop used to be faster.

My laptop didn't use to be this slow.

You can do this with almost any sentence or idea. It's a simple and quick exercise that takes no more than one or two minutes. You can also do it anywhere. The more you practise, the faster and better you become.

It really helps you to express yourself perfectly. But it also helps you find vocabulary in your head while you speak. This is a great skill to have and will help prevent those moments in a conversation when you don't know what to say.

This is most useful for expressing feelings and emotions. There are many different ways to express basic feelings and emotions like happiness or tiredness. This tends to be the same in most languages.

It's normally in these situations that you feel you don't express yourself as well as you could. That's normally because there are many different degrees of emotions. Take, for example, the sentence *"I'm hungry"*. *"I'm hungry"* often doesn't reflect exactly how you feel. There are different levels of hunger and to express yourself perfectly, you need to know which one is how you feel right now.

I'm a bit peckish.

I'm quite/pretty/really/so hungry.

I'm starving.

I'm famished.

I could eat a horse.

And there you have all the different levels of hunger that you need to express yourself perfectly.

Start today by finding as many different ways as you can to express feeling happy or tired.

In the beginning, practise with sentences about feelings and emotions. You will learn a lot of new vocabulary and you will start to express yourself perfectly every time someone asks you the simple question, "How are you?"

Day 30

To become an advanced English speaker, you don't need advanced vocabulary. Often, you need a wide variety of simple vocabulary to answer simple questions like the one above.

Expressing yourself perfectly doesn't mean you can say long and complicated sentences.

It means you can express more with fewer words.

REVIEW

- *Is it easy for you to start a new habit? Why/why not?*
- *Which tip from this chapter do you think will help you most in starting a new habit?*
- *How can you make the new habit easy to keep in the beginning?*
- *How can the practice plan help you keep the habit?*
- *What situations do you have most problems expressing yourself in?*
- *What feelings and emotions do you have trouble expressing?*
- *What can you do to rectify those problems?*

Plan

Practise

Review

Reward

DAY 31

HOW TO PUT IT ALL TOGETHER

"You now know that you are capable of doing incredible things, so go and do incredible things."

When you first start learning to play the guitar, it can feel tricky. What's difficult is the physical aspect of doing many things at the same time.

Each hand is doing something completely different and moving in different directions. On each hand, each finger is pressing or plucking strings in a particular order.

It feels as if you are juggling with too many balls, and all your effort goes into thinking about what each hand is doing.

But when you learn to play your first song well, all the different elements fit together perfectly and they all feel like a single action.

The hands and fingers move easily, naturally and effortlessly in a single action. The result is a beautiful song that you create with your hands.

All you need to do after that is repeat and enjoy the same results.

This is exactly the same process that you will need to go through to create a similar system to master English. It's a new habit, and it won't feel yours until you make it yours.

After 31 days, you understand exactly what you need to do, why you need to do it and, more importantly, how to do it. The only difference between today and tomorrow is that today, I am with you.

TOMORROW, YOU WILL BE ON YOUR OWN.

Your priority from tomorrow onwards is to make this new habit yours.

You need to practise the habit of being an independent English learner. Practise putting all the pieces together so they flow easily, naturally and effortlessly in a single habit.

When all the pieces are together in a comprehensive way, you only need to repeat and enjoy the results that it is guaranteed to give you.

Let's start to put it all together in a comprehensive way using my **PPRR** system.

1. **Plan**

   Planning is the most important part of making learning easy and effortless. **Plan** what you will learn and practise over the coming week using your **DNA-Plan**. Identify language that you have difficulty using and have it as your main focus for the coming week. Plan every bit of **practice** and add each one to your **practice plan** for the coming week. Write exactly **what** you will do, **when** you will do it and **how much** you will do. Make all the decisions once per week, so you never have to make a single decision during the week. Your plan makes the whole process **automatic**.

2. **Practise**

   This is where all the action happens. *The Big 3* should always be part of your daily practice. These three practice exercises are easy, massively effective, and they should always be part of your daily practice. They are **reading** novels, **general and specific listening**, and **fluency practice**. Reading, listening and speaking. The combination of these three forms the foundation of your contact with English. By doing this daily, you master the three most important **skills** and learn lots.

   But of course, you also need to learn specific language too.

Day 31

On top of The Big 3, you need to dedicate some time to **learning specific language**. This is **relevant** language that you identified while speaking, reading or listening. Language that you make mistakes with or language that you want to say but you don't know how. Use your **DNA-Plan** to decide how to learn it, then add it to your plan. Do **focused** and **unfocused drills** to **practise** the language that you want to learn. Practise the language using the skill that you consider your biggest **weakness**.

Your practice plan is your **short-term goal**. You should also set a **mid-term goal** and **long-term goal** to make sure you continue to make **progress** over the months.

3. **Review**

    Take a few minutes at the end of every day to **review** your day. Use the review questions to ask yourself what went well today, what didn't go so well, and what you could do better tomorrow. This way, you will make each day better than the previous, and it will show in your results.

    Review your **progress** every week and every month using the **progress check** questions. Ask yourself what progress you are making towards your **goals**, and what you could improve. **Check** your progress, then **modify** or **change** the process.

    With every answer to each review question, you make your process stronger and more efficient. Your **results** will get **better and better**.

4. **Reward**

    This only takes a few seconds, but is very important. It's your one moment to **focus** on all the **positive** aspects of the day. Feel **proud** of yourself and what you achieved today. Recognise the small steps you have taken that will move you closer to your goals. The brain will want to continue if it sees that what you are doing brings **positive feelings** and results.

    All this **positive thinking** reinforces the **habit** and will help make it **stronger** and more permanent.

It also puts you in the right frame of mind for the next day, makes you more **productive**, and gets you ready and **motivated** for tomorrow.

Well done!

Then wake up the next day and repeat the whole process. Focus on one day at a time. Don't focus on the end goal. Know that if you do what you know you need to do every day, the end result will be that you achieve all your goals.

Motivation, self-discipline and habit keep the system together. Stay motivated, improve your self-discipline and maintain the habit.

If you don't follow a comprehensive system, you will continue to feel frustrated. You will walk around with no aim and make little progress.

If you follow this system, you will master English, achieve all of your goals and you will be in control of the whole process.

You will become unstoppable.

Day 31

PRACTICE

HOW TO NEVER BE FRUSTRATED IN ENGLISH

"Today is not when it all ends. Today is when it all begins."

"All good things come to an end", as the old saying goes. When something good finally comes to an end, it's your responsibility to make sure something better begins.

"Out with the old and in with the new", as the other old saying goes.

Stop doing what you know doesn't work and start doing what you know works.

The only person who can do that is you.

It's 100% your responsibility.

Nobody is coming to help you.

But don't think that is negative. It's actually very positive. It means it all depends on you. It depends on what you do and how you do it.

It's what you do with the tools you now have that will decide how much progress you make. Know that you can do absolutely anything that you put your mind to.

You control your own progress.

WHY DO ENGLISH LEARNERS GET FRUSTRATED?

Because they don't make progress and they don't feel that they are in control of their own progress.

Learner frustration comes from not making progress and not being in control.

ALWAYS MAKE PROGRESS. ALWAYS BE IN CONTROL.

If you do this, you will achieve all of your goals in English. Success is inevitable.

If you follow the tips I have shown you, you will achieve anything you want in English.

Every English learner that follows my advice gets the results that they want and achieves the goals that they set.

I have never met a single student that has implemented the techniques I teach and not got the results that they wanted.

That doesn't mean that everybody achieves everything they want. Only the ones that follow the advice.

Only the ones that apply the techniques get the results.

If you apply these techniques, you get massive results.

The practice part is the easiest. What's difficult is keeping a habit, planning and thinking long-term.

All your effort should go into that.

The **PPRR** system is the most powerful tool you have to make sure you get there. It removes all the negative aspects of the journey and gives you full control over everything. Without it, you can get lost easily. With it, you will never get lost, and you will always be going in the right direction.

The only reason I wrote this book was to end learner frustration. I see frustrated learners every day, and it breaks my heart knowing that their frustration is completely avoidable.

The only thing I want and the only thing I care about is that my students make progress.

Everything else is secondary.

Day 31

Your destination is English fluency and mastery. Plan exactly how you get there, check your progress continuously, and change your route if you need to.

But keep walking. As long as you keep walking, you will get there. If you fall over in your journey, don't worry. Just make sure you stand up again and start walking. Right now, it's time for you to start walking on your own.

I remember my last day in France as if it were yesterday.

My two best friends and I spent my last full day at one of their houses. Then we stayed the night together in a teepee that he had in a field that his family owned. We spoke about the good times and laughed late into the night.

In the morning, we woke up, left the teepee and stood in the field. It was a beautiful summer morning, the grass was covered in dew and the sun was strong in our morning eyes. I quickly gave them both a big hug, said *"Au revoir"* and left.

It felt really strange because it wasn't a big farewell. It was as if we were going to see each other again at school the next day.

But of course, we didn't.

Later that day I felt sad. It felt as if everything had finished. It felt as if it were the end of something big.

But in fact, it wasn't.

That day was the start of my life.

My time in France had given me everything it could give and now it was time to start my own journey and find my own way.

Now it's time for you to make your own journey.

You have just read 66,912 words in English. Only 184 to go.

Well done you!

That's an incredible achievement.

Now the question is, what are *you* going to do with those words?

I ask you because I can't ask anybody else. It all depends on you. You have an incredible opportunity, but it all depends on what you do with that opportunity. From the smallest details to the biggest goals.

You now know everything you need to master English on your own.

WHERE DO YOU GO FROM HERE?

It's entirely up to you. You can go anywhere you decide.

This may be the end of the book, but it's the start of something much better.

It doesn't end today. Today is when everything begins.

You now know you are capable of achieving incredible goals.

So go and achieve incredible goals.

REVIEW

- *What are you going to do now?*

Plan: What, when and how you are going to practise.

Practise: Have good quality contact with English.

Review: Think about what you have learned today, what you have improved and what could be better.

Reward: Congratulate yourself and think about your achievements so far.

WHAT ARE YOU GOING TO DO NOW?

Here is something you can do to put everything you have learned into practice. Join *The How To Community*: a private community of independent English learners. It is full of people who have read this book and now have control of their learning, just like you. *The How To Community* is designed for you to do two things only: speak more fluently and make fewer mistakes.

In the community you get:

- Two live masterclasses with me every week
- Daily practice exercises: grammar, dictations, reading, vocabulary, prepositions & phrasal verbs...
- Unlimited speaking practice
- Weekly challenges
- The chance to ask me all your questions and doubts in our live Q&A classes

Remember, knowing is nothing. Practising what you know is everything. Come and practise, and start making real progress. As you have already bought this book, you get 100% off your first month in The How To Community.

Go to <u>www.how-to-english.com/discount</u> and I will send you an email with a code to get 100% off your first month.

I'll see you inside!

Adam

AFTERWORD

I hope you enjoyed reading this book as much as I did writing it. If you follow my system, stay focused and disciplined, you will achieve incredible things on your journey to fluency as an independent English learner.

Just because you are now independent, that doesn't mean our relationship has to end here. I would love to continue to help you on your journey in any way that I can.

You can continue to learn from and enjoy my work on the following platforms.

- *First and foremost, subscribe to my newsletter on www.how-to-english.com, where you can find courses to help you make even more progress in English, as well as blog posts and podcasts.*
- *Subscribe to my YouTube channel "How To English", where I upload regular videos of classes, talks and advice for English learners.*
- *On a more personal level, please connect with me on LinkedIn, Instagram and Facebook.*

Before any of that, though, I would like to ask you one favour.

I ask that you leave an honest review on Amazon. This is very important as it helps me as an author to reach more people so that I can help others improve their English. Reviews help Amazon decide which books to recommend to other potential readers.

When you leave a review, you help me as an author, but you also help others find, read and enjoy this book, just as you have. Simply go into your Amazon account, go to "my orders", and then click to leave a review.

Thank you.

Made in the USA
Thornton, CO
09/08/23 08:43:15

33f13a46-3e38-40a3-8acc-70e139498f3eR01